DISCARD

tricks & treats

THE ULTIMATE HaLLoWEEN BOOK

tricks & treats

THE ULTIMATE

HaLLoween Book

DEBORAH HARDING

Reader's Digest

The Reader's Digest Association, Inc.
Pleasantville, New York/Montreal

A Reader's Digest Book

Art Director
Pamela Kageyama

Design Consultant
Jean Locke Oberholtzer

Photographers
Cathy Sanders
(Fun Foods)

Lawrence E. Cohen
(Festive Fashions and sewing close-ups)

All other photos
Tim Lee

Illustrators
Ruth Schmuff
Phoebe Adams Gaughan

Library of Congress Cataloging in Publication Data

Harding, Deborah
Tricks & treats the ultimate halloween book /Deborah Harding
p. cm.
ISBN 0-7621-0085-0
1. Halloween decorations. I. Title
TT900.H32H36 1998
745.5941'1—dc21 97-51754

Printed in the United States of America

This book is lovingly and
gratefully dedicated to
Lillyan Mae Greene
who helped to make every
day of my childhood
a reason to celebrate.

Contents

Introduction

There was a time, not too long ago, when Halloween was essentially a one-night celebration, but now it's a fall holiday that extends for 4-6 weeks and is the second most widely celebrated holiday after Christmas.

Start A Family Tradition

This book has been planned as a start-a-family-tradition book which means that it includes activities that several generations of family and friends can enjoy together. Take the time to simply relax and laugh and appreciate one another. At Halloween, the joy of planning and preparation is as important as the results. After all, no one's going to be too upset if a costume isn't a custom fit or if a jack-o'-lantern's mouth is slightly too big. And if not every cookie is picture-perfect, you can always eat your "mistakes."

To remember these good times, begin a make-a-memory scrapbook of this annual event and record your decorations, costumes, and recipes and then compare and add on each year. One of my friends takes a picture of her three daughters, in costume, next to the same toy pumpkin every year. When she started, one little girl was about the same size as the pumpkin. It's amazing to see how tall the girls have grown and how their choice of costumes has changed. Be sure to include lots of snapshots of the family working together. You'll be delighted to have this keepsake to refer to as the children grow up.

This book provides dozens of great ideas for easy-to-make costumes for kids, indoor and outdoor decorations, toys and gifts, bazaar items, fun foods and festive fashions for grownups.

Step-by-step instructions and patterns are included for each project and additional helpful hints are included in the General Directions, Chapter Eight.

Start early, right after school opens, and read this book together with your children, a chapter at a time—there are lots of pictures to look at. Let a different family member be in charge of each chapter. Make choices and decisions together as to which projects you want to accomplish this year. Plan ahead, assign responsibilities to different people, and set dates to get together and create your selected projects.

I hope that you'll have as much fun using this book as we did in producing it for you and that it's one that you'll enjoy for many years to come.

Deborah Harding

CHAPTER ONE

Signs of the Season

Have you noticed that soon after Labor Day, mysterious decorations start appearing on your neighbors' doors and lawns? Sometimes even swinging from trees?

Researchers tell us that this trend really caught on with the use of plastic leaf bags that fill up to look like jack-o'-lanterns. It was a cue to adorn the outside of your home as well as the inside. A pumpkin on a doorstep and a soaped window are simply not enough anymore.

Whether it's a bittersweet wreath to herald the fall harvest season, a whimsical scarecrow—not necessarily in the vegetable garden—or a colorful banner, almost every home has something on display. And often it reflects originality and a sense of humor.

Get in the Halloween spirit and be the talk of the neighborhood with do-it-yourself tombstones, yard art in the shape of a friendly ghost, and a variety of door decorations. Wreaths aren't only for Christmas.

Choose just one design—or make several—and invite friends over to visit your own happy "haunted house."

Smiling Scarecrow

You Will Need

$3/8$ x 36 inch (1 x 91.5cm) dowel, for crossbars

Cotton fabrics, 44 inches (112cm)-wide:
$1/4$ yard (.25m) orange, for head;
$3/4$ yard (.70m) muslin, for body top;
$5/8$ yard (.60m) turquoise, for shirt;
$1/2$ yard (.50m) denim, for pants;
$1/8$ yard (.15m) yellow, for sign;
scraps of black fabric, for face and
assorted colors for patches

$1/2$ yard (.50m) burlap, for hat

Raffia to use as "straw"

Polyester fiberfill, for stuffing

4 x 25-inch (10 x 63.5cm) piece of heavyweight fusible interfacing, for sign backing

Fabric glue

Black permanent ink felt-tip marker

1 yard (.95m) twine

Floral wire

Rubber bands

Tape

Saw

Scissors and pinking shears

Tracing paper for pattern

A whimsical Smiling Scarecrow bears season's greetings. Criss-cross wooden dowels for a base, make a fabric body, and an appropriate wardrobe. This scarecrow is 36 inches (91.5cm) high.

What to Do

Making the Body and Crossbars:
1 Enlarge the patterns for shirt, pants, and hat, and complete the half patterns. To do so, fold tracing paper in half and lay over pattern with the fold line along the long dash lines. Trace, cut out, and unfold pattern.
2 To make the upper body, use the shirt pattern to cut out 2 pieces from muslin. Place pieces together, with right sides facing and edges matching. Stitch along all but neckline edges and sleeve ends, leaving 1-inch (2.5cm) seam allowances. Do not turn.
3 Saw the dowel crosswise in half to form 2 dowels. Place one dowel down the neckline of the muslin upper body, the other through the sleeves. Working at the neckline, securely wrap the dowels where they meet with the floral wire. Stuff fiberfill into the upper body, all around the dowels.
4 For legs, cut 4 strips from muslin, each 4 x 8 inches (10 x 20.5cm).

Stitch 2 pieces together along both long edges and one short side, $1/2$ inch (1.3cm) from edges. Repeat with remaining pair. Stuff each leg and stitch opening closed. Attach legs, side by side to bottom edge of upper body with a straight stitch.

Making the Head:
5 Cut out 2 orange fabric rectangles 8 x 11 inches (20.5 x 28cm) for head front and back. For face, lay head front flat with short edges at top and bottom. Cut 1-inch (2.5cm) triangles from black fabric for eyes and nose and glue to center of head front. Use marker to draw a crooked smile.
6 Place head front and back together with right sides facing. Stitch $1/2$ inch (1.3cm) from long edges, leaving top and bottom edges open. Gather top tightly with a rubber band. Turn right side out. Place the head over the vertical dowel as it extends from the

upper body, and fill with fiberfill. Gather bottom edges of head with your fingers and wrap with 2 strands of 12 to 15 inch-long (30.5 to 38cm) floral wire to secure; leave wire ends long. Twist wire ends together in back, adding an extra loop to make a hanging loop for the scarecrow. Insert gathered edges of head into upper body neckline, and stitch to secure.

Dressing Your Scarecrow:

7 Use patterns to cut out shirt front and back from turquoise fabric in the same way you cut the upper body in Step 2. In a similar way, cut a pants front and back from denim. For patches, cut small rectangles from assorted fabric scraps, arrange on fronts of shirt and pants pieces, and stitch or glue in place.

8 Place shirt front and back together, right sides facing and edges even. Stitch along top and bottom of sleeves, and sides, leaving ½ inch (1.3cm) seam allowances. Turn right side out. Make a slit down center back and all across the shirt sleeves to enable you to place it over the upper body, then glue or stitch the back of shirt closed.

9 Place pants front and back together, right sides facing and edges even. Stitch along side and inseams, ½ inch (1.3cm) from edges. Turn right side out.

10 Cut slits into bottom edges of shirt, sleeves, and pant legs, to fringe them. Pull pants on over stuffed legs so shirt edges overlap the pants. Tie twine around waist, securing pants in place.

11 For a hat, use pattern to cut out 2 pieces. Sew or glue patches onto hat, then sew hat front and back together with right sides facing along all but the gently curved brim. Turn right side out and place on head. Turn up brim and glue or stitch to secure. Indent top of hat and unravel unsewn edges.

Finishing Touches:

12 Insert raffia between scarecrow's head and hat, gluing to secure. Wrap and tie raffia around neck. With remaining raffia, make 4 small bundles about 6 inches (15cm) long and secure one end of each with a rubber band. Insert banded end of one bundle into the end of each sleeve and pants leg; secure in place with glue and floral wire.

13 To make sign, fuse interfacing to back of yellow fabric. Using letters about 2½ inches (6.5cm) high, write "Happy Halloween" with felt-tip marker. Pink the edges of the fabric with pinking shears. Make a small hole at each end of sign and insert a strand of ribbon or yarn, then tie to the raffia "hands."

14 Hang your Smiling Scarecrow on a door, post or barn by placing the looped wire over a nail.

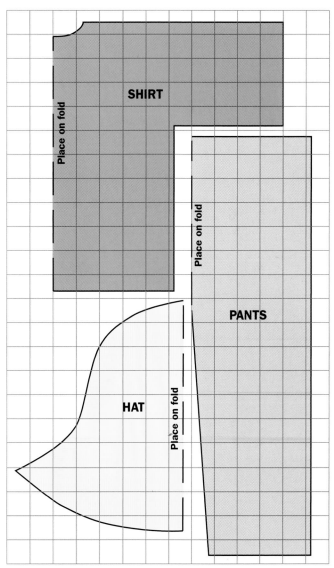

REDUCED PATTERNS FOR SCARECROW
Each square equals 1 inch (2.5cm).

Grave Yard

Halloween decorations can create a Grave Yard. These do-it-yourself tombstones are cut from Styrofoam® and spray-painted for that "neglected" look. Make up your own scary messages: initials, names, or choose one shown here.

You Will Need

Sheet of Styrofoam® plastic foam 36 x 12 x 2 inches (91.5 x 30.5 x 5cm)

Sharp knife

Candle stub or paraffin, to wax the knife

Craft knife #1

Spray paint in the following colors: black, silver, gray, plus moss green or light brown

Black felt-tip marker

Metal plant stakes or tent pins, plus hammer, for installation

What to Do

Cutting Directions:

1 Wax knife with an old candle or paraffin. Trim 6 inches (15cm) from one 36-inch (91.5cm) side of Styrofoam. Cut size will now measure 30 x 12 x 2 inches (76 x 30.5 x 5cm).
2 Refer to the photo for the different shaped tombstone tops. For a flat top such as "TOO SOON" no more cutting is required. For a top such as "TRICK OR TREAT" or "T.R. BONES," cut a 2-inch (5cm) square from each corner. For a rounded tombstone such as "BOO" or "R.I.P."' cut a 3-inch (7.5cm) triangle from each corner and then smooth the curve by sanding with a scrap of Styrofoam.

Decorating the Tombstones:

3 With the felt-tip marker, draw double-lined letters onto the foam to spell out names or short phrases as desired.

Most of the letters shown are about 5 inches (13cm) high. With the craft knife, cut into the drawn letters to make grooves about ¼ inch (6mm) deep. (You do not want to cut through the sheet.) Add scrollwork, cracks, or other design lines and cut grooves along those as well. In the same way, outline the tombstone with a continuous groove about 1 inch (2.5cm) from the edges along the sides and top.

4 Spray black paint into carved letters, scrollwork, and outline. Allow to dry.
5 Next, spray-paint the tombstone with silver, holding can at an extreme angle to cover the surface, but not the blackened grooves. When silver paint is dry, repeat lightly with gray paint. When gray is dry, spray along just one edge and onto one side with moss green or light brown, to give tombstone an aged, neglected look.

Setting Up the Tombstones:
6 For each tombstone, hammer 2 plant stakes or tent pins about 6 inches (15cm) apart halfway into the ground. Center tombstone over them, then push it down gently until it meets the ground. In windy weather, you may need to buttress tombstones with longer stakes or pickets propped behind.

Black Cats

Beware of Black Cats. This pair is made from corrugated plastic board. Make easel stands or tape cats to trees or porch columns.

You Will Need

Black, 4mm thick corrugated plastic board, 20 x 30 inches (51 x 76cm): one for each cat; plus an extra one, if desired, for easel stand

Large sheet of brown paper

Green cellophane wrap or plastic wrap, for eyes

Black electrical tape

1½ yards (1.4m) orange dot grosgrain ribbon

2 large jingle bells

Craft knife #1

White chalk

Yardstick

Optional: plant stakes

What to Do

1 Enlarge pattern on a sheet of 20 x 30 (51 x 76cm) brown paper and cut out. Use a few pieces of tape to secure the enlarged drawing to the plastic board.

2 Working over a cutting mat or protected surface, cut out the cat shape with a craft knife. Carefully cut out the eye holes. Repeat for second cat, but reverse the pattern to produce a mirror image.

3 Fold a large sheet of green cellophane or plastic wrap (folded in half, twice for extra thickness), and tape behind eye cutouts.

4 To make an easel stand for the back of each cat, use another sheet of plastic board. Using chalk and a yardstick, mark trapezoids 3 inches (8cm) at the top, 24 inches (61cm) in height, and 10 inches (25cm) at the base. Cut out the easel stands. Center easel stand on back of cat with bottom edges of easel stand and cat even and tape top edge of easel stand to secure. For extra stability, in a windy area, tape one or more plant stakes to the back of the cat to secure it in the ground.

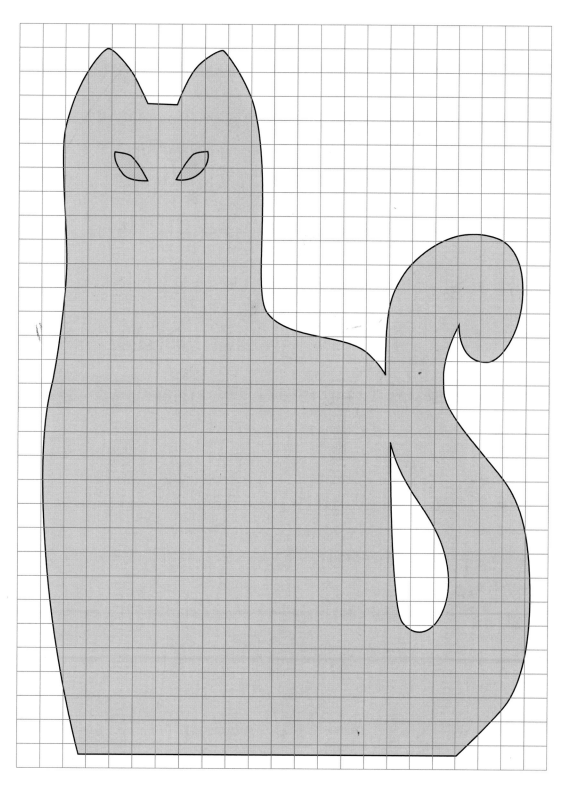

REDUCED PATTERN FOR BLACK CATS
Each square equals 1 inch (2.5cm).

Hanging Ghosts

Out on a limb is a trio of Hanging Ghosts. Transparent ghosts are made by winding glue-covered string around balloons and popping the balloon when dry. The long-skirted ghost, center, is a Styrofoam® ball wrapped with acrylic yarn.

You Will Need

For String Ghosts

1 balloon for each head

1 ball white household string

White glue

Skirt/suit hanger with 2 metal clips

Medium-size mixing bowl

Tweezers

Scraps of black and white felt for eyes and mouth

Nylon filament thread for hanging

For Yarn Ghost (center)

1 skein 100% acrylic worsted-weight yarn

1 Styrofoam® 4-inch (10cm) plastic foam ball, for head

Scissors

Scraps of black felt, for eyes and mouth

White glue

What to Do

For String Ghosts

1 Blow up one balloon for each ghost head, knot at the top. Hang balloon on hanger with metal clips (one hanger will hold two balloons).

2 Pour undiluted white glue into a bowl. Unwind and cut several yards of household string and place it in the glue until completely saturated. Pull out one end of glue-covered string and, starting at the top near the knot, begin winding string in all directions around balloon until the surface is evenly covered. If you run out of string, just start a new piece.

3 Allow string-covered balloons to dry at least 24 hours (longer in humid weather).

4 Pop the balloon. It's a good idea to do this outdoors or over a sink as there will be some debris from dried glue.

NOTE: Do not leave balloon fragments where young children might find them and swallow them.

5 With your fingers and/or tweezers remove any extra glue that is filling in the spaces.

6 Refer to the photograph for the features: For eyes, cut two ovals of black felt and glue in place. Add two smaller white ovals over the black ones. To cut shape for mouth, fold black felt in half. Cut a large U-shape; then cut a smaller U-shape inside it. Open felt and glue in place as shown in photo.

7 Tie ghosts to a tree branch with nylon filament thread.

For Yarn Ghost

1 Open skein of yarn and arrange it into a full circle. Cut completely through one side of skein. Cut a small strand of yarn and use it to tie the skein of yarn opposite the cut. Tie securely. If you haven't tied your strands tightly enough, tie a second strand around them. The original tie will hold the strands in place, so you should be able to tie the second strand tighter. Clip off any extra yarn.

2 Position tied end over plastic foam ball and pin in place.

3 Cut another strand of yarn and use it to tie yarn, under the ball, for the neck as shown in the photo. Fluff out body as much as possible and trim bottom ends as desired, these ends are left a little uneven on purpose.

4 From black felt, cut ovals for eyes and mouth and glue in place.

5 To hang, cut one more strand of yarn and loop through the knotted area at the top.

Bittersweet Branches

You Will Need

Styrofoam® plastic foam wreath form, 14-inch (35.5cm) in diameter

Floral wire

15 to 20 bittersweet branches (real or artificial) approximately 12 to 18 inches (30.5 to 46cm) long

Large package of sheet moss

Floral pins

White glue

What to Do

1 For a hanger, make a loop in the center of floral wire and insert wire ends into the back of the wreath form, about 3 inches (8cm) apart. Apply glue to areas where wire penetrates plastic foam, and let dry thoroughly.

2 Glue sheet moss to front surfaces of wreath form until it is completely covered.

3 Arrange bittersweet branches over front of moss-covered wreath form, and use floral pins to attach securely. Intertwine branches and pin down so they more or less follow the general wreath shape.

4 Glue bittersweet leaves over any floral pins which remain visible.

Just a few Bittersweet Branches and a wreath form are the basic ingredients for this handsome fall door decoration. You could also bring it indoors to use it flat, on a table, to frame a punch bowl.

Pole Cat Banner

Machine-stitch your own Pole Cat Banner from nylon fabric (sometimes referred to as ripstop or parachute nylon). Layer colored fabrics and tissue pattern, stitch them together, and then cut away fabric to reveal the design on both sides.

You Will Need

One piece of purple nylon 29 x 53 inches (73.5 x 135cm), for banner

One piece yellow nylon 27 x 28 inches (68.5 x 71cm), for outer moon

One piece orange nylon, 26 x 25 inches (66 x 63.5cm), for inner moon

One piece black nylon, 29 x 28 inches (73.5 x 71cm), for cat and fence

Tissue paper, 28 x 48 inches (71 x 122cm), for tracing pattern

Purple, orange, yellow, and black thread

Scissors

Pins

What to Do

Preparing the Banner:

1 Enlarge pattern and trace onto tissue paper.

2 Place tissue paper over purple fabric with bottom edges even. Place a few pins around the edges to secure. Place remaining nylon pieces *under* the tissue paper but *on top* of the purple fabric. Checking to see that the marked tissue outline falls within the edges of the corresponding fabric, position each remaining color in place where it will be used beginning with yellow under the outer moon, then orange under the moon, then black under both the cat and fence. At this point, pin through pattern and all fabrics to hold everything in place.

Stitching the Banner:

3 Using small straight stitches machine-stitch through all layers (including the tissue paper) and outline each section of the banner motif. When all lines are stitched, remove pins and gently tear away tissue paper.

4 Trim off all the excess fabric close to the straight stitching.

5 Using thread to match the color of the shape, satin-stitch around each shape over all of the straight stitching and raw edges.

6 Turn the banner over and carefully trim away the purple nylon in the center of each shape to expose the correct color of the motif. Trim any excess fabrics concealing the design.

7 To hem all around turn under ½ inch (1.3cm) on each long side and one short side of purple fabric. Stitch in place. To make a casing, turn under 3 inches (7.5cm) on remaining short end and topstitch in place, leaving the ends open for inserting a flagpole or slat.

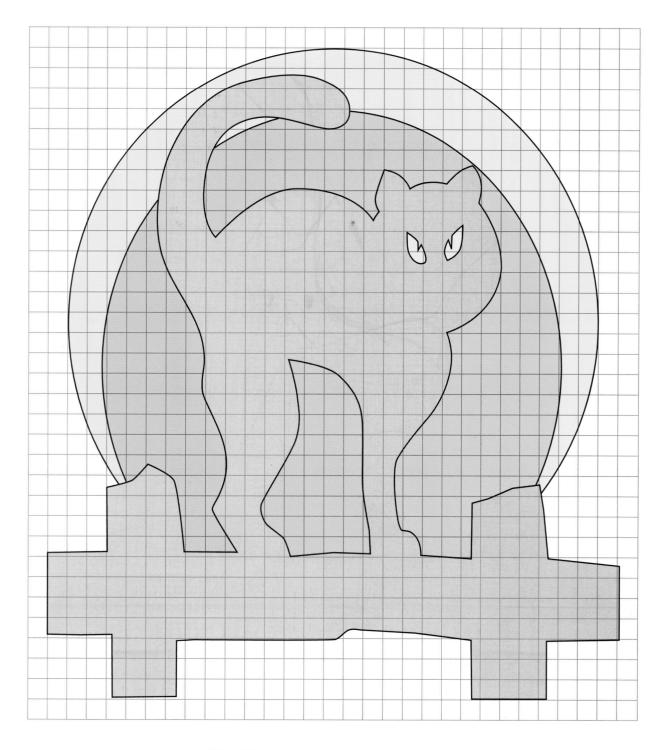

REDUCED PATTERN FOR POLE CAT BANNER
Each square equals 1 inch (2.5cm).

Going Batty Wreath

T he whole family will want to join together to make this Going Batty wreath. Children can wrap colorful acrylic yarn around Styrofoam® shapes and then cut out the felt details. Parents can help them glue the faces in place and then hot-glue the finished decorations to a grapevine wreath form covered with excelsior.

You Will Need

Styrofoam® plastic foam shapes: one 4-inch (10cm) disk, for the moon behind the bat; seven 2$\frac{1}{2}$-inch (6.5cm) balls, for cats and jack-o'-lanterns; two 1$\frac{1}{2}$-inch (3.8cm) eggs, for bat bodies

Grapevine or other sturdy wreath form, 16 inches (40.5cm) in diameter

Package natural-color excelsior (or other fake straw), to cover wreath

Chenille pipe cleaner, for hanger

100% acrylic worsted-weight yarn, to cover Styrofoam® : 1 skein each orange, black, and yellow

Felt: three 9 x 12-inch (23 x 30.5cm) sheets black, for bats' wings and ears, cats' ears, and pumpkin faces; 5 x 6-inch (12.5 x 15cm) piece brown, for pumpkin stems; 3-inch (7.5cm) square yellow, for eye glints; 2 x 11-inch (5 x 28cm) piece of bright green, for pumpkin leaves; small scraps of apple green for cats' eyes and bats' mouths

6 small (4mm) wiggle eyes, for bats

Two $\frac{1}{2}$-inch (1.3cm) orange pompoms for cats' noses

9 x 12-inch (23 x 30.5cm) piece of paper-backed fusible web

2 sets animal whiskers (or broom straws), for cats

Pencil, ruler, tracing paper

Scissors

Rolling pin

Toothpicks, for spreading glue

Hole punch

Sharp or serrated knife

Candle stub or paraffin, to wax knife

Wire cutters

Thick tacky glue

Glue gun and glue sticks

What to Do

Preparing the Wreath:

1 Make a hanging loop with chenille pipe cleaner and twist ends together. Wrap ends securely into wreath form on the back.

2 Arrange excelsior over all front surfaces of the wreath. Use a glue gun to secure it in place.

Preparing Black Felt:

3 Fuse paper-backed web to one side of a black felt sheet. Peel off the paper backing, and fuse to a second sheet of black felt. Set this aside for bats' wings and ears and cats' ears.

Making the Moon:

4 For front surface, bevel edges of disk on one side by rolling along the edges with a rolling pin.

5 Cover plastic foam shape with yellow yarn as follows, using thick tacky glue. Start by adhering one end of yarn to the flat back of the shape. Wrap yarn all around shape, wrapping over the glued end to hold it in place. Continue wrapping until shape is completely covered and no foam shows through. Cut yarn and glue the remaining end to the back.

Making the Bats:

6 Wax the knife with a candle stub, or paraffin, and cut plastic foam eggs lengthwise in half. You will use 3 of the 4 halves.

7 Following Step 5 but using black yarn, cover each egg half.

8 For wings, fold tracing paper in half and place over half wing pattern, page 24, with long dash lines along the fold. Trace pattern and cut out; unfold. Pin open wing pattern to fused black felt, and cut out 3 complete wing pattern pieces. Trace and cut out patterns for bat ears as well.

9 Center a body, with flat surface down and the narrow end of egg shape at the bottom, on each wing piece. Glue with glue gun to secure.

10 Referring to the photo for position and using tacky glue, add features to bats: Cut 2 ears from unfused black felt; glue with straight ends along back of top of body. For eyes, use a hole punch to make 2 yellow felt circles and glue in place. Glue a wiggle eye on top. For a mouth, tie 4 knots close together on a short strand of orange yarn and trim ends beyond knots. Glue knotted strand to face in an inverted "V." Cut a tiny triangle of light green felt, for tooth and glue to center of mouth.

Making the Jack-O'-Lanterns:

11 Following Step 5 but using orange yarn, cover 5 Styrofoam balls. There is no flat surface so wherever you glue the final yarn end will be the back.

12 For stems, cut five $\frac{5}{8}$ x 6-inch (1.5 x 15cm) strips of brown felt. For each, begin at a short end, roll strip tightly, and secure at end with glue. Glue one to each orange ball.

13 Trace patterns for leaf, eyes, noses, and mouth on tracing paper and cut out. Notice that, on photo, if eyes are circles, noses are triangles and vice versa. Pin patterns to felt and cut 5 leaves from green felt; 5 mouths, 9 triangles, and 6 circles from unfused black felt. With a hole punch, make 10 small circles from yellow felt.

14 Referring to photo for positions, glue a leaf beside each stem, and glue on eyes, nose, and mouth, inverting mouth for either a smile or a frown. Glue on yellow circles for glints in the eyes.

Making the Cats:

15 Following Step 5 but using black yarn, cover 2 balls. Since there is no flat surface for the back, wherever you glue the final yarn end will be the back.
16 Trace patterns for ears and eyes. Cut 4 ears from remaining fused black felt. For eyes, cut 4 ovals from yellow felt, 4 circles from light green, and a very thin strip from unfused black felt. Referring to photo, page 22, glue pieces in place.
17 Glue on whiskers, with a pompom nose in between.

Assembling the Wreath:

18 Make sure wreath hanger is at the top. Referring to the photo on page 22, arrange and hot-glue decorated shapes to wreath, with the moon behind one of the bats.

PATTERNS FOR GOING BATTY WREATH
Actual Size

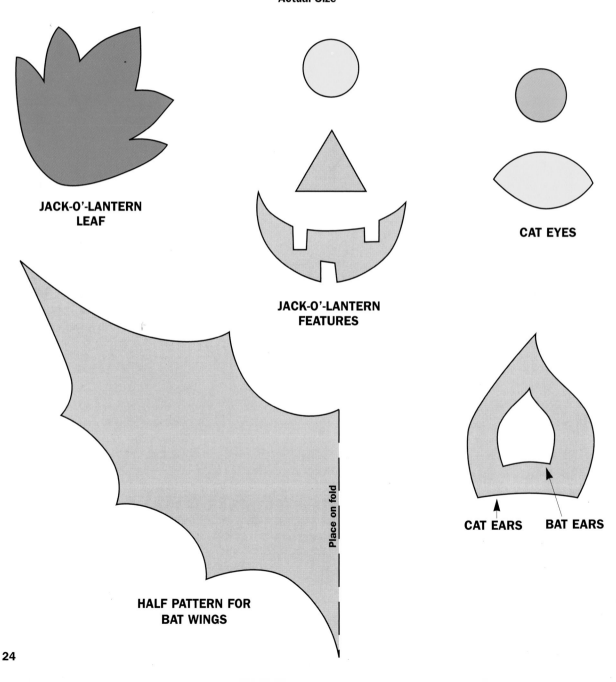

JACK-O'-LANTERN
LEAF

JACK-O'-LANTERN
FEATURES

CAT EYES

CAT EARS   BAT EARS

Place on fold

HALF PATTERN FOR
BAT WINGS

Creepy Crawlies

These little spiders are actually quite endearing. Creepy Crawlies can be displayed almost anywhere indoors or out. Try suspending several, on nylon threads, from a porch ceiling. Let each guest cut down their favorite monster to adopt as a pet.

You Will Need

Styrofoam® plastic foam balls for spider bodies and heads:
3 and 4 inch (7.5 and 10cm)
for each large spider;
2½ and 3 inch (6.5 and 7.5cm)
for each medium spider;
2 and 2½ inch (5 and 6.5cm)
for each small spider

1 inch (2.5cm) Styrofoam® plastic foam balls for spider feet:
4 for each spider

Eight 9mm black chenille
pipe cleaners, for legs

2 wiggle eyes: 24mm for large,
18mm for medium,
and 15mm for small spiders

Strip of self-stick plastic doll eyelashes

Black acrylic paint

Scraps of felt: red for mouths
and pink for cheeks

White glue

Sharp or serrated knife

Candle stub or paraffin,
to wax the knife

Paintbrush

Round toothpicks (these have sharper
tips than the flat kind)

What to Do

Preparing the Body:

1 To join the balls for the head and body, press them together, rotating them slightly to sand them flat where they meet. Brush off the loose crumbs of plastic foam. Insert a toothpick to join the balls, adding glue before pushing them all the way together. To enable the spider to lie on a surface without rolling, press the larger ball onto the table to slightly flatten its underside.

2 For feet, use a waxed knife and cut each of the the 1-inch (2.5cm) balls in half.

3 Paint all foam pieces black. In order to paint all surfaces of the feet at once, skewer each ball or half-ball on a toothpick, paint, and insert other end of toothpick into a scrap piece of plastic foam, a corrugated cardboard box, or an inverted egg carton until paint is dry.

Adding the Legs:

4 Trim the length of the pipe cleaners as follows: to 8½ inches (22cm) for large spider, to 6½ inches (16.5cm) for medium spider, and to 5½ inches (14cm) for small spider.

5 When paint is dry, use a toothpick to poke 8 leg holes, 4 on each side of the spider body. Position the holes so that the legs will extend outward horizontally from the body. Place a drop of glue on each hole and push a pipe cleaner leg into the hole. Use a toothpick to poke a hole into the rounded surface of each foot. Adding glue, push opposite end of leg into hole made in foot. Allow glue to dry.

6 Bend legs as shown in photo so that the spider will stand.

Making Faces:

7 Glue wiggle eyes on head. Cut small strips of plastic doll eyelash and glue across the center of the wiggle eyes. Paint the wiggle eyes above the lash with black paint, for eyelids. From felt, cut small pink circles, for cheeks, and small red lip shapes or semicircles, for a mouth. Glue these pieces in place.

Yard Art Ghost

This friendly Yard Art Ghost welcomes trick-or-treaters and guests. It's cut from foamcore with a craft knife. If you're handy with a jigsaw, the pattern could also be adapted to ¼-inch (6mm) plywood.

You Will Need

30 x 40-inch (76 x 102cm) sheet of white foamcore board

Duct tape

Orange and yellow acrylic paint, for candy corn

Heavy black felt-tip marker, for mouth and lettering

Green cellophane or green plastic wrap, to fit behind eyes

Wire clothes hanger

Craft knife #1

Needle nose pliers, wire clippers

Paintbrush

Colored chalk

Optional: plant stakes

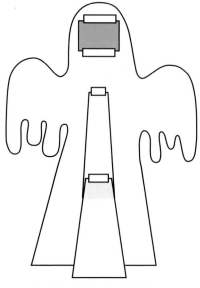

BACK VIEW OF GHOST

What to Do

1 Enlarge patterns and trace onto brown paper or newspaper and cut out. Using chalk, trace around patterns onto foamcore. Or merely refer to reduced pattern as a guide and draw shapes freehand on foamcore board, using chalk. Ghosts are meant to be irregular in shape, so there is really no need to duplicate this design exactly, but if you are not pleased with your outlines, erase the chalk with a tissue and redraw.

2 Working over a cutting mat or protected surface, cut out the shapes for ghost, sign, 2 candy corns and 2 easel-back stand pieces along their outlines with a craft knife. Carefully cut out the eye holes.

3 Paint wide tops of candy corn with yellow paint. Paint middle sections with orange paint. Let dry and paint the reverse side and edges. Use chalk, then black marker to draw a smile on the ghost and letter the sign to read "Welcome."

4 Use a single sheet of cellophane or a sheet of plastic wrap folded in half for double thickness, and tape behind eye cutouts.

5 Make an easel stand to support the ghost at the back. Overlap the 2 easel pieces along shaded areas, tape together securely with duct tape. Position bottom of stand even with ghost bottom. Center and tape top of stand to ghost as shown in back view (left).

6 Untwist hook of hanger and bend wire out straight. Use wire cutters to cut hanger in half and use pliers to introduce a crimp or curlicue off-center. With pieces right side down, arrange ghost, sign and candy corn as shown in photo and connect with hanger wire, taping along the back of the foamcore pieces to secure.

7 Set ghost in a covered area such as on a porch. If necessary, use additional duct tape to secure ghost cutout to porch floor or to keep it from blowing over. If standing on the ground, you may want to insert plant stakes into the dirt and tape them to the back of ghost to hold it steady.

NOTE: Since the largest surfaces of foamcore board are paper, avoid leaving ghost in an unprotected area for extended periods of time.

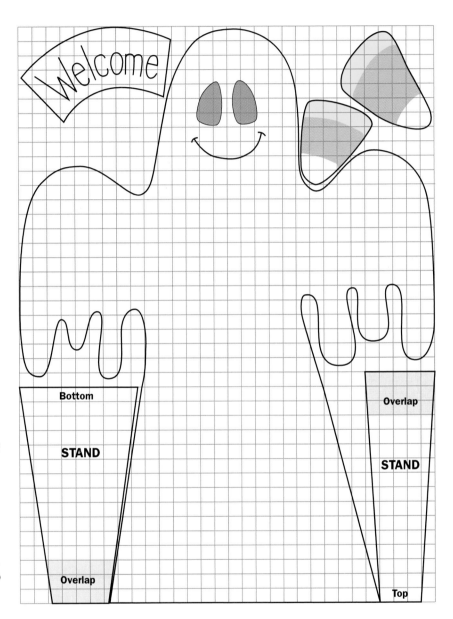

REDUCED PATTERNS FOR YARD ART GHOST
Each square equals 1 inch (2.5cm).

CHAPTER TWO

Costumes for Kids

O nce upon a time youngsters dressed up in costumes, on just one night a year, for a couple of hours of neighborhood trick-or-treating. That's certainly not the case these days. Children enjoy showing off their costumes at school, at home, and at friends' houses.

With that in mind, here's a collection of costumes that are easy for parents to make and fun for kids to wear. Add touches of machine embroidery such as that on the scarecrow and the ballerina, create golden wings for an angel, or simply cut out felt spots and iron them to a white sweat suit as with the dalmatian. You'll find that several of these ideas are appropriate for other occasions: The angel could be used for a Christmas pageant and the ballerina outfit is perfect for a dance-class recital.

Most important, make this a family affair. Let the kids participate. Dad or Granddad can help with some of the shopping, and this may be the perfect opportunity to ask your mother or a next-door friend how to master the decorative stitches on your sewing machine. Make an event out of a fitting—perhaps a "conference" over hot chocolate. It doesn't matter if every stitch is perfect or every seam is straight. The only thing that matters is the delighted smile on your child's face when he or she sees the finished result.

Take a snapshot of your little trick-or-treater and start a family scrapbook.

Top Dog

This adorable costume is a blessing for busy moms who don't sew. All you need is a hooded sweat suit, black felt, and fusible webbing to iron the spots in place. Children will want to draw the spots and cut them out themselves: There's no right or wrong pattern, any size and shape is just fine.

There are also spots on the gloves and you could tape some to the sneakers as well. Ears and tail are made from white felt. For a tighter fit around the neck, tie on a red bandanna or use a piece of ribbon for a "collar." The nose and whiskers are drawn on with face paint.

Top Dog

You Will Need

White hooded sweat suit

$1/2$ yard (.50m) black felt, for spots

$1/2$ yard (.50m) white felt, for ears and tail

1 yard (.95m) heavy-duty, paper-backed fusible web to apply spots

Glue gun or needle and thread to attach tail and ears

Small amount of polyester fiberfill (or tissue paper), for stuffing the tail

Pencil or marker

White gloves

Scissors (manicure scissors are helpful for rounded shapes)

Iron

What to Do

Making the Spots:

1 Fuse paper-backed web to one side of black felt. Draw irregularly shaped circles for spots on the paper side. Spots range in size from $1/4$ inch (6mm) to $2 1/2$ inches (6.5cm). It doesn't matter if no two are alike. This costume should have about 100 spots on the pants and tail and about 75 spots on the top, including the ears.

2 Cut out the spots.

3 After removing paper backing from the spots, fuse them in place on the sweat suit.

Making the Ears:

4 For each ear, cut 2 pieces of white felt 7 x 4 inches (18 x 10cm). Cut same-size fusible web and fuse felt pieces together.

5 Trace around pattern (below) on white felt and cut out ear shape. Repeat for second ear.

6 Fuse spots to one side of each ear.

7 Glue (or sew) ears to either side of hood.

Making the Tail:

8 Cut a piece of white felt 10 x 14 inches (25.5 x 35.5cm).

9 Begin rolling one long side toward the other long side. Before first roll is completed, insert fiberfill or tissue paper, lengthwise, for stuffing. Continue to roll tightly. Secure finished roll with glue.

10 Glue on spots.

11 Secure tail to back of pants with a glue gun or sew in place.

Finishing Touches:

12 Cut additional black felt spots and fuse, or glue, to white gloves.

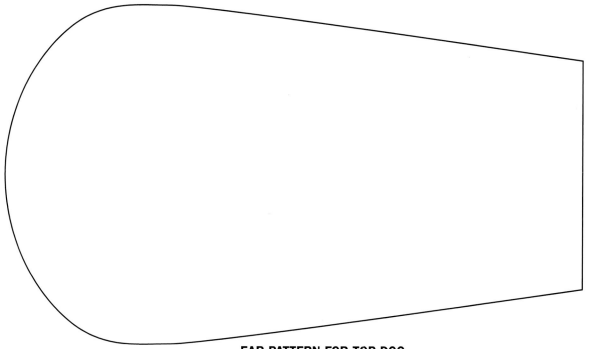

EAR PATTERN FOR TOP DOG
Actual Size

Fantasy Fly

A sweat suit and a headband are the secret ingredients in making this costume. The stripes on the front of the body and the legs are applied with fabric paint. Glitter glue also works well. In this case, the stripes on the sleeves are stitched in place. Mom was going to appliqué the stripes on the front of the shirt as well, but Christopher decided that he wanted faster results and helped with the painting. Stripes on sleeves can also be painted. As this is a "fantasy" insect, let your youngster make up whatever markings he or she wants. Wings attach to the back of the sweatshirt with Velcro®.

Fantasy Fly

You Will Need

Green sweatshirt and sweat pants

Green glitter paint

Small paintbrush

Tube of black glitter paint

$^1/_2$ yard (.50m) green metallic fabric, if you sew on arm stripes

$^1/_2$ yard (.50m) lightweight paper-backed fusible web, if you sew on arm stripes

$^3/_4$ yard (.70m) of Velcro® black hook-and-loop tape, to attach wings

Fabric glue

2 black pipe cleaners for antennae

2 Styrofoam® balls 1 $^3/_4$ inch (4.5cm) in diameter, for antennae

Plastic headband

Scrap of black felt for covering the headband

Fabric marker

Thread

Scissors

Iron

What to Do

Decorating the Pants:
1 To paint stripes on the legs, lay the pants on a flat surface and insert folded paper (newspaper will do) into the legs.
2 With fabric marker, draw outlines of 2 stripes on the front of each pants leg approximately 2 x 10 inches (5 x 25.5cm) long (see photo).
3 Beginning with green glitter paint, and paintbrush, paint *inside* the drawn lines. When the green paint dries, outline the stripes with the black glitter paint. Repeat for back if desired.

Decorating the Top:
4 Place the sweatshirt on a flat surface with folded paper inside the chest area. Draw diagonal stripes approximately 2 x 11 inches (5 x 28cm) and paint as in Step 3.

To add stripes to the sleeves, continue to decorate with paint or fuse and stitch them in place as we did.

5 To paint the sleeves, insert paper into each sleeve and paint 3 horizontal stripes on the front of the sleeves first. When dry, repeat on the back of the sleeves, joining up stripes.
6 To appliqué stripes in place, carefully open side seams from the waistline hem to cuff and spread shirt flat. Draw 6 stripes 2 x 11 inches (5 x 28cm) on the paper side of the fusible web. Fuse web to wrong side of green metallic fabric and cut out stripes. Remove paper and fuse 3 stripes to each sleeve. Use a

zigzag stitch to outline the edge of each stripe. With right sides together, re-stitch side seams, being sure to catch the ends of the stripes in the seams.
7 Stitch an 8-inch (20.5cm) piece of the loop side of hook-and-loop tape vertically to the center back of the sweatshirt. Stitch another 3-inch (7.5cm) piece of loop tape just below each shoulder seam on the back of the shirt. (Remaining tape will be attached to the wings.)

To make the wings, see page 37.

Making the Headpiece:
8 Measure the headband and cut a piece of felt $^1/_2$ inch (1.3cm) longer and wider than this measurement. Center the felt over the headband and glue in place. Wrap the edges of the felt strip to the underside of the headband and secure with glue.
9 Paint Styrofoam balls with green glitter paint and let dry.
10 For antennae, wind pipe cleaners around large magic marker to form spirals. Glue one end of each pipe cleaner to headband and insert remaining ends into Styrofoam balls.

My Little Angel

This good-as-gold angel looks as if she's just been sprinkled with stardust. Begin with a ready-made shirt and combine gold-and-white patterned netting and iridescent white lamé for the layered skirt with more gold-and-white netting for the bodice. Then add sparkling gold sequins to the waistband and the neck and cuffs of the shirt. The lightweight gold lamé wings are attached to the bodice, which crisscrosses in front and meets at the sides with Velcro®. This angel applied her own makeup, consisting of gold star stickers. Her halo is a garland of gold stars, but gold tinsel could also be used.

My Little Angel

You Will Need

2 pieces of white tulle
72 x 18 inches (183 x 46cm),
for bottom layer of skirt

2 pieces of iridescent white lamé
72 x 18 inches (183 x 46cm),
for middle layer of skirt

2 pieces of white-and-gold patterned
netting, 72 x 18 inches (183 x 46cm),
for top layer of skirt

1/8 yard (.15m) white satin,
for waistband

3/4 yard (.70m) Velcro®
hook-and-loop tape

2 pieces of white-and-gold patterned
netting, 4 x 38 inches (10 x 96.5cm),
for bodice

2 yards (1.85m) gold sequins,
for trimming skirt and shirt

1 package star garland for halo

White shirt

Scissors

Pins

Tape measure

Thread

What to Do

Making the Skirt:

1 To make the waistband, measure the child's waist and cut a piece of satin to waist measurement plus 4 inches (10cm) long x 4 inches (10cm) wide.
2 To create the V-shaped hemline, cut 24 deep inverted "Vs" approximately 3 inches (7.5cm) deep and 3 inches (7.5cm) wide into one long edge of each 72 x 18-inch (183 x 46cm) piece of tulle, lamé, and netting.
3 Layer skirt fabrics as follows: white tulle on bottom, iridescent fabric in middle, and white/gold netting on top. Keeping the long straight edges even, stitch 2 rows of machine basting along the straight edge.
4 Pull basting stitches to gather the skirt. Pin skirt to the right side of one long edge of the waistband. Beginning and ending 1/2 inch (13mm) in from each short edge, stitch in place and remove the pins.
5 Fold the waistband in half, lengthwise, with right sides together, and stitch the short ends.
6 Turn the waistband to right side and slipstitch the remaining long edge in place.
7 Stitch a 4-inch (10cm) piece of hook-and-loop tape to each end of the waistband. Trim waistband with sequins and glue them in place.

Making the Bodice:

8 Stitch 2 rows of machine-basting in each short edge of the 4 x 38 inch (10 x 96.5cm)-wide pieces of tulle as shown in Figure A.

Pull on the basting stitches to gather the tulle to a width of 2 inches (5 cm).
9 Stitch hook tape of hook-and-loop tape to one end of each tulle piece and loop tape to the opposite end of each tulle piece.
10 Stitch an additional row of gathering across each strip of tulle 8 inches (20.5cm) up from one end.

Make the wings, page 37.

11 Fold tulle strips in half, lengthwise, and mark the midpoints.
12 Following Figure B, crisscross the nongathered halves of the tulle. Stitch the tulle to the front of the wings at the marked midpoints. Gather the tulle softly as you stitch. Stitch the tulle a second time 4 inches (10cm) from the end of each piece as shown.
13 To fit the wings, cross the loose (gathered) ends of the tulle across the child's chest and join to corresponding hook-and-loop tapes.

Finishing Touches:

14 Trim neck and sleeves of shirt with sequins and stitch, or glue, in place.
15 Twist star garland into a circle to form a halo.

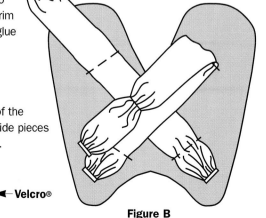

Figure B
ASSEMBLY DIAGRAM FOR ANGEL BODICE AND WINGS

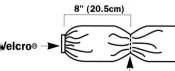

8" (20.5cm)

Velcro® →   ← Velcro®

Gathered

Figure A
PREPARING TULLE STRIP FOR ANGEL BODICE

Wings for Angel and Fly

You Will Need

FOR MY LITTLE ANGEL

2 yards (1.85m) gold lamé fabric

3 yards (2.75m) medium-weight interfacing (white)

Thread to match

4 yards (3.70m) medium- to heavy-weight pliable wire

Wire cutters

FOR FANTASY FLY

2 yards (1.85m) sheer black fabric

3 yards (2.75m) medium-weight interfacing (black)

Thread to match

1/2 yard (.50m) green metallic fabric, for stripes on wings

1/2 yard (.50m) lightweight paper-backed fusible web

4 yards (3.70m) medium to heavy-weight pliable wire

Wire cutters

Remaining hook-and-loop tape

Iron

What to Do

Cutting Directions for Wings:

1 Enlarge pattern for half wing section (facing page). Place pattern on fabric with long dash lines along fold. Trace around pattern and cut out. Open cut fabric and you will have one full wing section. Repeat for back of wings.

2 Cut 2 more of these wing sections from interfacing.

Assembling the Wings:

3 Baste interfacing wings to wrong side of fabric wings.

4 Place wings, right sides of fabric together, and stitch around the outer edge with a 1/2-inch (1.3cm) seam allowance, leaving an opening in bottom of wings for turning as shown in Figure A. Trim seam and turn wings right side out.

5 To make a casing for the wire, stitch 3/8 inch (1cm) from the edge of the wings all around.

6 Cut 2 pieces of wire 45 inches (114.5cm).

7 Slide wire into each side of the wings through the casing and mold to shape, if necessary. After wire is completely inserted, slipstitch opening closed.

Adding Stripes to Fly's Wings:

8 On paper side of fusible web, draw 6 stripes 2 x 13 inches (5 x 33cm).

9 Fuse web to wrong side of green metallic fabric. Cut out stripes along marked lines.

10 Fuse 3 stripes, vertically, to the front of each wing. Outline stripes with a zigzag stitch.

Attaching Fly's Wings:

11 Stitch an 8-inch (20.5cm) piece of hook tape to center front of wings, matching up with the piece of loop tape at center back of sweatshirt.

12 Attach the wings, positioning them so that stripes show to best advantage. Mark placement for remaining pieces of hook tape so that they are opposite the loop tape at shoulders.

Optional for Angel:

Glue narrow gold tinsel roping to edge of wings.

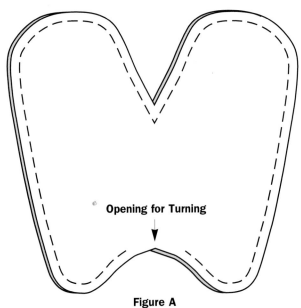

Opening for Turning

Figure A
ASSEMBLING WINGS

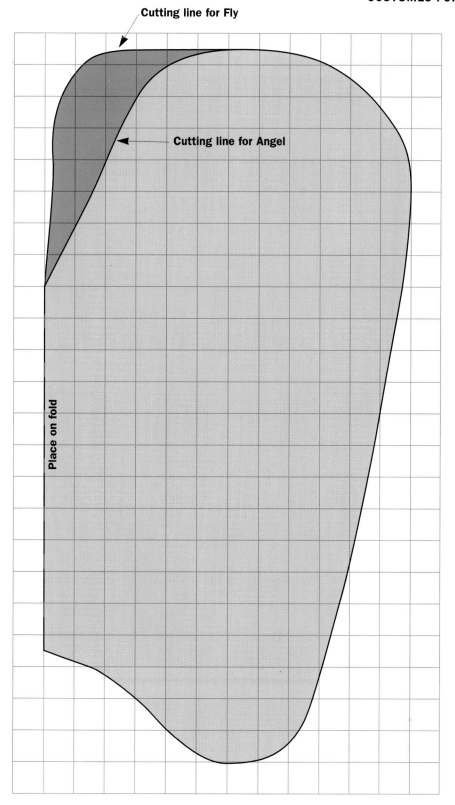

Cutting line for Fly

Cutting line for Angel

Place on fold

REDUCED PATTERNS FOR ANGEL AND FLY WINGS
Each square equals 1 inch (2.5cm).

Prima Ballerina

Every little girl wants to have a ballerina costume—especially one that's made just for her. Shop together for pastel-colored tulle to make the full skirt. Designed in three tiers, it stitches up quickly on a sewing machine. A blue ribbon waistband and streamered bow, at the back, complete the picture-perfect effect. The motifs on the leotard are, appropriately, machine-embroidered ballet slippers. And like all aspiring ballerinas, Brianne (shown above) wanted to wear her hair up, so a tulle hair decoration was made to match the tutu. This is a costume that your little dancer will want to wear again and again.

Prima Ballerina

You Will Need

1 piece of pink tulle 24 x 7 inches (61 x 18cm), for underskirt

3 pieces of tulle 50 x 5 inches (127 x 12.5cm) in each of the following colors: white with pink embroidery, pink, and light blue, for tiers of skirt

2 ¹/₄ yards (2.10m) 1 ¹/₂ inch (3.8cm)-wide light-blue grosgrain ribbon, for waistband bow and streamers

4 inches (10cm) Velcro® hook-and-loop tape, for waistband

Leotard

Tear-away fabric stabilizer (for machine-embroidery on leotard) or purchased appliqués

2 pieces of tulle 24 x 12 inches (61 x 30.5cm), for hair scrunchy

6 inches (15cm) ¹/₂ inch (13mm)-wide elastic, for hair scrunchy

Scissors

Matching thread

Tape measure

Pins

What to Do

Making the Skirt:

1 Finish one long edge of each 50 x 5-inch (127 x 12.5cm) piece of tulle using a narrow zigzag stitch or serger-rolled hem.

2 Layer tulle as follows: one layer of white/pink on top, one layer of pink in middle, and blue on the bottom. Stitch 2 rows of machine basting along remaining long edge.

3 Repeat with remaining 6 tulle pieces. You will have 3 sets of 3 layers each.

4 Gather each layered tulle set along basted edge.

5 Using the 24 x 7-inch (61 x 18cm) pink tulle for an underskirt, sew layered sets of tulle in separate tiers wedding-cake style. Begin by sewing the first tier to one long side of tulle for the top; sew a second tier in the middle, and then sew remaining layered set/tier to bottom edge of pink tulle.

6 Cut 2 pieces of ribbon 24 inches (61cm) long. Sandwich the top edge of the skirt between the 2 pieces of ribbon and pin in place. Stitch around all the edges of the ribbon.

7 Stitch hook side of hook-and-loop tape to one end of the waistband and the loop side of the tape to the opposite end of the skirt.

8 Tie remaining ribbon into a streamered bow and tack in place to outside back of waistband.

Decorating the Leotard:

9 Mark the desired locations for embroidery, or appliqué motifs, on front of leotard as shown in the photograph.

10 Back leotard with stabilizer and machine-embroider ballet slipper motifs or stitch on ready-made appliqués.

Making the Hair Scrunchy:

11 Cut zigzags in each long edge of the 2 pieces of tulle 24 x 12 inches (61 x 30.5cm).

12 Place these 2 pieces of tulle together and fold in half lengthwise. Create a casing by stitching ³/₄ inch (2cm) from the folded edge.

13 Insert the elastic through the casing and secure at each end with a pin. Fold tulle in half, bringing the short ends together, and stitch with a ¹/₄-inch (6mm) seam allowance. Remove pins.

"Patchy" the Scarecrow

Here is one little scarecrow that isn't intended to frighten anyone away (but maybe we shouldn't tell him that?). The top is a circular cape cut from burlap. Patches are made out of pumpkin print and solid-color fabrics, which are pinked around the edges and then stitched in place. Special touches include Halloween-motif appliqués on the patches. Use the ready-made variety or machine-embroider them in place. Patchy's pointy, green, brimmed hat repeats some of the same designs. Straw is attached to the inside of the hat with masking tape, secured to the top at arm level, and then tucked into the cuffs of the jeans. Justin helped by cutting and taping patches to his jeans and supervising the placement of the straw. Substitute black felt for the cape and hat, and these directions could easily be adapted for a witch costume.

"Patchy" the Scarecrow

You Will Need

1 ¹/₄ yards (1.15m) of tan burlap, for cape

¹/₂ yard (.50m) of green burlap, for hat and patches

Scraps of black felt and Halloween-print fabrics, for patches

Paper-backed fusible web

¹/₂ yard (.50m) Halloween-print fabric, for hat lining and patches

Straw or raffia, for hat and arms and cuffs of jeans

Thread for embroideries*

Tear-away stabilizer for embroideries*

*for use with machine embroidery

(additional scraps of Halloween-print fabrics and/or store-bought appliqués if not using machine embroidery)

Pinking shears

Scissors

Small snap

String and pencil (or fabric marker)

Masking tape

NOTE: This size cape fits most 3 to 4-year-olds. For an older child, you may need to draw a larger circle.

What to Do

Cutting Directions for Cape:

1 Cut a 38-inch (96.5cm) square of tan burlap.

2 Fold the burlap in half (Figure A). Then fold in half a second time, bringing short edges together: You will have a 19-inch (48.5cm) square.

3 Cut a piece of string about 20 inches (51cm) long and tie around a pencil until there are 19 inches (48.5cm) remaining. Hold loose end of string at folded corner of fabric. Referring to Figure B, pull string taut and draw a curved line at the raw edges of the square.

4 Then, following Figure C, draw a second curved line 3 inches (7.5cm) down from the folded corner, to create a neck opening. Draw the jagged edge of the cape as indicated in the illustration and photograph. Cut out cape along drawn lines.

5 From felt, burlap, and Halloween-print fabrics, using pinking shears, cut out as many patches as you wish for front and back of cape. The ones shown here are 7-, 3-, and 1-inch (18, 7.5, and 2.5cm) square. There are also a few triangles (half squares cut on the diagonal).

Making the Cape:

6 Machine-embroider felt patches if desired. (Machine-embroidery motifs used here are the smiling ghost on the larger black patch and the carrot-nose, green-hatted scarecrow.)

7 Open cape and lay on a flat surface. Draw a 4-inch (10cm) line out from the small center circle (neck opening) toward the edge as shown in Figure D. Cut along this line.

8 Set sewing machine to zigzag stitch. Stitch around small circle (neck opening). Hand-stitch snap in place at close of circle.

9 Position all patches on cape. Pin and then stitch in place.

10 Try cape on child to determine where his or her arms will be and mark location on fabric. With masking tape, attach straw, in place, at markings.

Finishing Touches:

11 With masking tape, tape patches to blue jeans.

12 Tuck straw in cuffs of blue jeans.

DIAGRAMS FOR SCARECROW CAPE

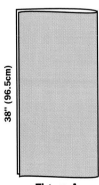

Figure A

38" (96.5cm)

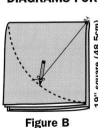

Figure B

19" square (48.5cm)

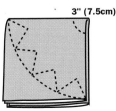

Figure C

3" (7.5cm)

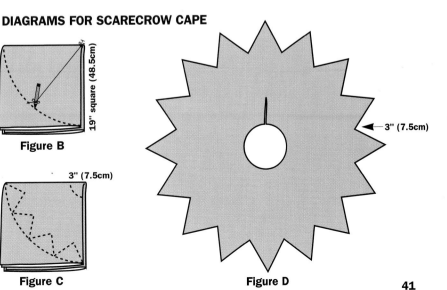

Figure D

3" (7.5cm)

Siegfried the Sorcerer and the Fairy Princess

N
o special magic is required to stitch up these striking outfits. The Sorcerer's cape is two rectangles of satin that are stitched together and then machine-appliquéd with silver lamé stars. Our handsome young model, Justin, wears it over a silver lamé vest. Justin's hat is painted with freehand stars and spirals, a step that kids can do themselves. Ashley, the Fairy Princess, is also wearing a lined satin cape. The construction for these two capes is similar except that by stitching the casing for the ribbon drawstring further down on the Princess' cape, it creates a collar effect. Her silver lamé crown is encrusted with paste-on jewels. And yards of silver sequins outline the edges of the cape and the waistband of her dance-length tulle skirt. Both costumes have matching drawstring goodie bags sized to hold a generous supply of treats and party favors.

Siegfried the Sorcerer

You Will Need

1 $^1/_2$ (1.40m) yards purple satin,
for cape and hat

1 yard (.95m) turquoise satin,
for cape lining

1 yard (.95m) silver lamé,
for vest and stars

$^3/_4$ yard (.70m) lining fabric, for vest

$^1/_2$ yard (.50m) paper-backed fusible
web, for appliqués

$^1/_2$ yard (.50m) fusible fleece, for hat

12 inches (1.85m) Velcro®
hook-and-loop tape

2 yards (1.85m) $^1/_2$ (1.3cm)-wide
purple ribbon

Silver glitter paint

Paintbrush

Tissue paper

Scissors

Tape measure

Iron

What to Do

Cutting Directions for the Vest:

1 Enlarge the vest patterns (following page) onto tissue paper.
2 Fold silver lamé in half. Pin pattern for back to fabric with long dash lines on fold. Cut one. Cut 2 vest fronts. Repeat with lining fabric.

Making the Vest:

3 With right sides of vest fronts to right side of vest back, stitch the shoulder and side seams of the vest together with a $^1/_2$-inch (1.3cm) seam allowance.
4 With right sides facing, stitch vest lining together at the shoulder and side seams, leaving an opening in one side seam.
5 With right sides together, stitch vest and lining together around the outside edges and armholes. Trim seams to $^1/_4$ inch (6mm). Turn the vest right side out through the opening in the lining. Slipstitch the opening closed.
6 Stitch a 3-inch (7.5cm) piece of hook-and-loop tape to each side of the center front of the vest for closing.

Cutting Directions for the Cape:

7 Cut one piece of purple satin and a matching one of turquoise satin 43 x 31 inches (109 x 79cm).

8 Cut a $^1/_4$-yard (.25m) piece of silver lamé. Using pattern (following page), trace 12 stars to paper side of fusible web and fuse to the wrong side of the silver lamé. Cut out stars.

Making the Cape:

9 Remove paper backing from stars and fuse them to the right side of purple satin.
10 Using a zigzag stitch, machine-stitch around the edges of each shape.
11 With right sides of purple and turquoise satin together, stitch around the 2 short sides and one long side. Begin and end $^3/_4$ inch (2cm) down from the top edge, as shown in Diagram for Sorcerer's Cape (below). Stitch along top edge, leaving a 5-inch (12.5cm) opening for turning. Turn right side out and slipstitch opening closed.
12 Measure down $^1/_2$ inch (1.3cm) from top edge of the cape and draw a line. Stitch along marked line to form casing. Cut a 1-yard (.95m) piece of ribbon and insert the ribbon through the casing.

To make the hat, see page 45.

Making the Goodie Bag:

13 Cut 2 pieces of turquoise satin 10 x 13 inches (25.5 x 33cm).
14 With right sides together, stitch around 2 long sides and one short side of bag.
15 Turn under $^3/_4$ inch (2cm) at the top edge of the bag and stitch, leaving an opening at one side seam for inserting the ribbon.
16 Using silver glitter paint, paint stars and swirls on bag.
17 Allow paint to dry; insert ribbon through casing.

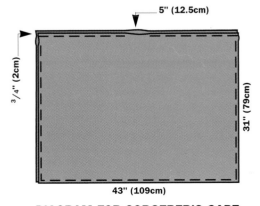

5" (12.5cm)

3/4" (2cm)

31" (79cm)

43" (109cm)

DIAGRAM FOR SORCERER'S CAPE

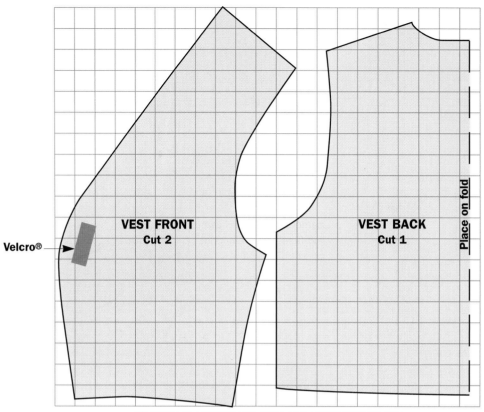

REDUCED PATTERNS FOR SORCERER'S VEST
Each square equals 1 inch (2.5cm).

Velcro®

VEST FRONT
Cut 2

VEST BACK
Cut 1

Place on fold

Actual Size

PATTERN FOR STAR APPLIQUÉ

Hats for "Patchy" the Scarecrow and Siegfried the Sorcerer

Cutting Directions for the Hats:

1 Measure the circumference of your child's head and enlarge hat pattern below until the bottom edge of the hat equals half the measurement plus 1 inch (2.5cm). For example, if the child's head measurement is 20 inches (51cm), then the bottom edge of the hat pattern should measure 11 inches (28cm).

2 For scarecrow only, enlarge the brim until its circumference equals the bottom edge of the hat pattern so that these 2 pieces fit together.

3 Before cutting out hat, fuse fleece to the wrong side of the Halloween-print fabric for scarecrow and to the wrong side of the silver lamé fabric for sorcerer.

4 For scarecrow only, peel away paper and fuse Halloween-print lining to green burlap. Fold fused fabrics, lining side up.

5 For sorcerer only, fold both the silver lamé fabric and the purple satin separately, right sides facing.

6 Place enlarged pattern piece(s) on folded fabric with long dash lines on fold. Trace and cut out. For scarecrow, you will have one fused piece for the top and another for the brim. For sorcerer, you will have one silver lamé piece and one purple satin piece.

Making the Scarecrow Hat:

7 Cut patches for the hat 3 inches (7.5cm) and 1 inch (2.5cm) square.

8 Machine-embroider patches or add purchased appliqués.

9 Topstitch patches in desired locations.

10 With right (burlap) sides together, stitch back seam of hat, using a ½-inch (1.3cm) seam allowance. Turn hat right side out.

11 Machine-baste 1 inch (2.5cm) in from inside edge of brim. Make clips every 2 inches (5cm) along basted line.

12 Starting at center back seam, topstitch top of hat to brim, using a zigzag stitch, lining side of brim against burlap side of hat. Trim away excess fabric. Topstitch back opening of brim closed with a zigzag stitch.

13 With masking tape, attach straw to inside of hat at sides.

Making the Sorcerer's Hat:

14 Paint freehand stars and swirls on right side of purple satin with silver glitter paint. Allow paint to dry thoroughly.

15 With right sides facing, stitch purple and silver hat pieces together, using a ½-inch (1.3cm) seam allowance and leaving an opening for turning. Turn hat right side out and slipstitch opening closed. You will now have a flat, wedge-shaped piece.

16 Roll wedge shape into a cone. Cut a 9 ½-inch (24.3cm) length of the hook side of hook-and-loop tape and attach to one side of center of hat; cut an equal length of loop tape and attach to opposite side of hat.

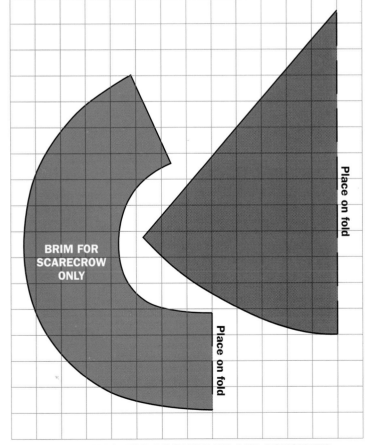

BRIM FOR SCARECROW ONLY

Place on fold

Place on fold

HAT PATTERN FOR SCARECROW AND SORCERER
Each square equals 1 inch (2.5cm).

Fairy Princess

You Will Need

1 ³/₄ yards (1.60m) magenta satin
for cape, waistband, and bag

1 ¹/₂ yards (1.40m) pink satin,
for cape lining

2 pieces of tulle
2 x 28 inches (183 x 71cm),
in each of the following colors:
light pink, dark pink, white, for skirt

¹/₂ yard (.50m) silver lamé, for crown

Assorted fake gems for crown

2 yards (1.85m) ³/₈ inch (1cm)-wide
pink ribbon, for cape and bag

¹/₂ yard (.50m) fusible fleece, for crown

6 yards (5.50m) silver sequins,
for cape and waistband

8 inches (20.5cm) Velcro®
hook-and-loop tape for skirt

Pins

Thread

White glue

Tape measure

Scissors

Fabric marker

Iron

What to Do

Cutting Directions for the Cape:
1 Cut one piece of magenta satin and a matching one of pink satin 34 x 43 inches (86.5 x 112cm). This includes the collar.

Making the Cape:
2 Stitch pink and magenta satin, right sides together, starting at center top. As shown in Figure A, leave a 1-inch (2.5cm) opening 5 inches (12.5cm) down on the right side. Continue sewing all around, leaving a corresponding 1-inch (2.5cm) opening on the opposite (left) side. Leave an opening, center top, for turning.
3 Turn the cape right side out and slip-stitch opening closed.
4 To create the collar casing, draw two horizontal lines across the cape connecting the small openings in each side seam (Figure B). Stitch along these marked lines.
5 Glue sequins on all edges of the magenta side of the cape, below the casing. Glue sequins to all edges of the pink side of the cape above the casing.
6 Insert 1 yard (.95m) of ribbon through the casing.

Making the Skirt:
7 To make the waistband, measure your child's waist and cut a piece of magenta satin to waist measurement plus 4 inches (10cm) long by 4 inches (10cm) wide.
8 Layer the tulle as follows: light pink on bottom, white in middle, dark pink on top. Stitch 2 rows of machine basting along one long edge of tulle through all layers.
9 Gather tulle and pin to the right side of one long edge of the waistband, and stitch in place. Remove the pins and fold waistband in half lengthwise

with right sides together and stitch the ends. Turn the waistband right side out and stitch remaining long edge in place (the top edge of the tulle will now be enclosed in the waistband).
10 Stitch a 4-inch (10cm) piece of hook-and-loop tape to each end of the waistband. Using your fabric marker, draw intersecting circles across the front of the waistband. Glue sequins along the drawn lines.

Making the Crown:
11 Measure your child's head. Enlarge the pattern in Figure C until the bottom edge of the crown equals the circumference of the head *plus* 4 inches (10cm). Using the pattern, cut out 2 pieces of silver lamé and one piece of fusible fleece.
12 Fuse fleece to the wrong side of one crown piece. With right sides together, stitch crown pieces using a ¹/₄-inch (6mm) seam allowance and leave an opening in the bottom edge for turning.
13 Trim the excess fabric at the points and turn the crown right side out. Slipstitch the opening closed. Topstitch close to edges of crown.
14 Sew a 3-inch (7.5cm) piece of hook-and-loop tape to each end of the crown, hook side to wrong side of crown, loop side to right side of crown.
15 Glue the gems to front of crown as shown in the photograph.

Making the Goodie Bag:
16 Follow steps 13–17 for the sorcerer's bag on page 43, but do not paint. Optional: You may wish to glue gems and sequins on the bag.

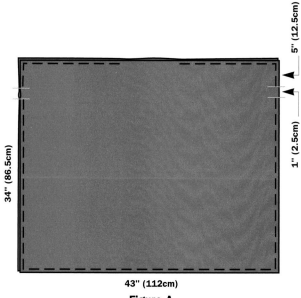

Figure A
DIAGRAM FOR FAIRY PRINCESS' CAPE

43" (112cm)

34" (86.5cm)

5" (12.5cm)

1" (2.5cm)

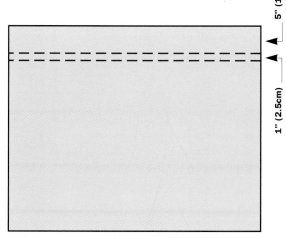

Figure B
CASING DIAGRAM FOR PRINCESS' CAPE

5" (12.5cm)

1" (2.5cm)

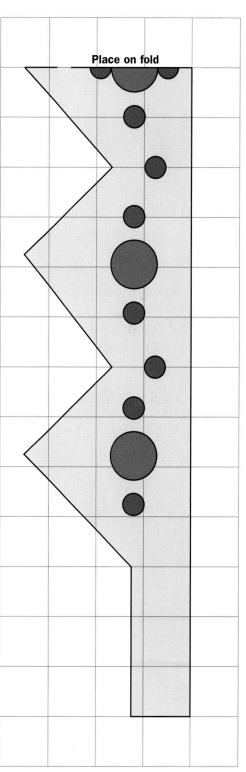

Place on fold

Figure C
REDUCED PATTERN FOR PRINCESS' CROWN
Each square equals 1 inch (2.5cm).

Buzzy the Bumble Bee
& Jackie-O'-Lantern

At first, we guessed that Michael might want to be the jack-o'-lantern, but he soon informed us that "boys just want to be bugs" and was delighted with his choice of a bee. He painted the Styrofoam® balls for the antennae while his mother ironed on the black felt stripes on the body sections. Our little pumpkin had a chance to put her artwork to good use by drawing the face for the front of her costume, which is also ironed on. The bottoms of both fleece costumes are gathered with elastic and the tops are tied together with a ribbon drawstring closing. Basic directions for the two are similar but the collars and headpieces vary. If you want a plumper effect, stuff tissue paper or polyester fiberfill in the body area. However, most children prefer this less bulky version, which allows them to sit comfortably, run around, and join in games without restriction.

Buzzy Bumble Bee

You Will Need

1 ³/₄ yards (1.60m) yellow fleece, for body

³/₄ yard (.70m) black felt, for stripes

1 yard ³/₈-inch (1cm)-wide black ribbon, for neck edge

1 yard ³/₈-inch (1cm) wide elastic, for bottom edge

1¹/₂ yards (1.40m) black tulle, for collar

Black and yellow thread

³/₄ yard (.70m) paper-backed fusible web, to attach stripes

2 Styrofoam® balls, 1³/₄ inches (4.5cm) in diameter, for antennae

2 black pipe cleaners, for antennae

Plain headband

Black glitter paint

Paintbrush

Pins

Scissors

Tape measure

Fabric marker

Straight edge

Glue gun

Iron

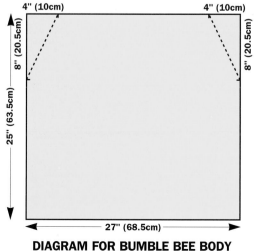

DIAGRAM FOR BUMBLE BEE BODY

(Diagram labels: 4" (10cm), 4" (10cm), 8" (20.5cm), 8" (20.5cm), 25" (63.5cm), 27" (68.5cm))

What to Do

Cutting Directions for Body and Stripes:

1 Cut 2 rectangles each 27 x 25 inches (68.5 x 63.5cm) from yellow fabric.

2 Fuse webbing to back of felt and cut out 8 stripes each 27 x 2 inches (68.5 x 5cm).

3 From black tulle, cut 8 pieces each 54 x 5 ½ inches (137 x 14cm).

Making the Bumble Bee Body:

4 To make armholes, measure down 8 inches (20.5cm) along each 25-inch (63.5cm) edge of each yellow rectangle and mark fabric. Then measure in 4 inches (10cm) along the top edges of the rectangles and mark. Draw a line connecting the marks on each side, as shown in Figure A, and cut along the lines.

5 To position stripes, measure 8 inches (20.5cm) down from the top on the right side of each yellow rectangle. Draw a horizontal line the width of the fabric. Draw 3 more lines spaced 5 inches apart. Remove the paper backing from the back of the stripes, center the stripes over marked lines, and fuse in place.

6 Turn under a ½-inch (1.3cm) hem along each armhole and press. Topstitch hems in place.

7 To make collar layer 4 tulle pieces, and gather together along one of the long edges. Repeat with remaining 4 tulle pieces. Pin tulle to top edge of the front and back of the body pieces, adjusting gathers to fit. Baste in place.

8 Turn under ½-inch (1.3cm) casing along the top edge of front and back. Stitch in place. With right sides together—and tulle collar inside— stitch front to back at sides, with ½-inch (1.3cm) seam allowance.

9 Insert black ribbon through the top casing for a drawstring closing.

10 Turn under ½-inch (1.3cm) casing at bottom edge and stitch, leaving a 3-inch (7.5cm) opening for inserting the elastic.

11 Cut elastic to 29 inches (73.5cm). Insert the elastic through the casing and overlap elastic ends by 1 inch (2.5cm). Stitch ends of elastic together.

12 Have your child step into the costume through the top. Gather the neck edge by pulling the ribbon and tie in place to secure.

Making the Headpiece:

13 Measure headband and cut a strip of black felt ½ inch (1.3cm) longer and wider than measurement. Center felt over headband and glue in place. Wrap edges of felt strip to underside of headband and secure with glue.

14 Paint Styrofoam balls with black glitter paint and let dry.

15 Glue one end of the pipe cleaners to the headband and insert the other ends into the Styrofoam balls.

Jackie-O'-Lantern

You Will Need

1³/₄ yards (1.60m) of orange fleece, for body

1 yard (.95m) of ³/₈-inch (1cm)-wide green ribbon, for neck edge

1 yard (.95m) of ³/₈-inch (1cm)-wide elastic, for bottom edge

¹/₂ yard (.50m) green fleece, for leaves

1 piece of brown felt 6 x 3¹/₂ inches (15 x 9cm), for stem

¹/₄ yard (.25m) black felt, for face

¹/₄ yard (.25m) paper-backed fusible web, for face

Plain headband

Pipe cleaner

Scissors

Tape measure

Glue gun

Iron

What to Do

Cutting Directions for Pumpkin Body and Face:

1 Cut 2 rectangles each 27 x 25 inches (68.5 x 63.5cm) from orange fabric, for body.

2 Trace around patterns on green fleece and cut out 8 small leaves and 4 large leaves (facing page).

3 Fuse webbing to back of black felt. Draw triangles for eyes, nose, and a jack-o'-lantern mouth on paper side of fusible web. Cut out along drawn lines.

Making the Pumpkin Body:

4 Remove paper from black felt features and fuse them to the right side center of one of the orange rectangles for the front of the costume.

5 Refer to the diagram on page 51. To make armholes, measure down 8 inches (20.5cm) along each 25-inch (63.5cm) edge of each orange rectangle and mark fabric. Then, measure in 4 inches (10cm) along the top edges of the rectangles and mark. Draw a line connecting the marks on each side, as shown, and cut along the lines.

6 Turn under ¹/₂ inch (1.3cm) along each armhole and press. Topstitch hems in place.

7 Stitch 2 same-size leaf pieces, right sides together, with a ¹/₄-inch (6mm) seam allowance, leaving the wide end of leaf open. Turn leaf to right side. Repeat this process with remaining leaf pieces. When you are finished, you will have 4 small leaves and 2 large leaves.

8 Baste one large leaf and 2 small leaves (large leaf in center) to top edge of body front. Repeat for back.

9 Turn under ¹/₂-inch (1.3cm) casing along the top edge of front and back. Stitch in place. With right sides together—and leaves inside—stitch front to back at sides, with ¹/₂-inch (1.3cm) seam allowance.

10 Insert green ribbon through the top casing for a drawstring closing.

11 Turn under ¹/₂-inch (1.3cm) casing at bottom edge and stitch, leaving a 3-inch (7.5cm) opening for inserting the elastic.

12 Cut elastic to 29 inches (73.5cm). Insert the elastic through the casing and overlap elastic ends by 1 inch (2.5cm). Stitch ends of elastic together.

13 Have your child step into the costume through the top. Gather the neck edge by pulling the ribbon and tie in place to secure.

Making the Headpiece:

14 Cover headband with green fleece. Cut out 12 small leaves. Join and complete leaves as in the collar. Glue or sew 6 finished leaves to headband, forming a circle.

15 To create stem, begin at one short end of brown felt and roll up tightly. Glue remaining end in place. Insert a pipe cleaner into center of stem, trim even with the stem.

16 Glue or stitch stem to center of leaves.

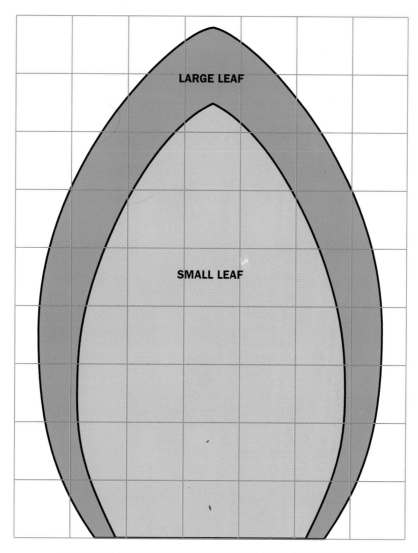

LARGE LEAF

SMALL LEAF

REDUCED LEAF PATTERNS FOR JACKIE-O'-LANTERN
Each square equals 1 inch (2.5cm).

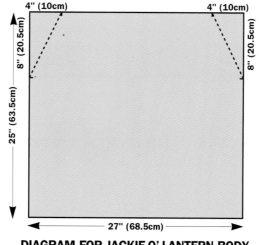

4" (10cm)   4" (10cm)

8" (20.5cm)   8" (20.5cm)

25" (63.5cm)

27" (68.5cm)

DIAGRAM FOR JACKIE-O'-LANTERN BODY

Marvelous Makeup Tricks

Some parents have concerns about how safe it is for children to wear masks which can limit their seeing clearly—and being seen—especially when crossing the street. It's also true that many masks can become hot and uncomfortable after a period of time, and make it difficult to gobble candy corn and dunk for apples. Therefore, makeup is the best solution! It enables the wearer to "remain in disguise" throughout all the festivities without a bothersome object covering the face or head.

For some tricks-of-the trade ideas, we turned to Michael R. Thomas, a makeup artist who specializes in creating fabulous made-up faces for kids in movies, TV, and real life. Michael explains that it's simpler than you think. Using ordinary ingredients you probably already have in your kitchen and bathroom cabinets—or the face-paint makeup that's available for children this time of year—you can create cute or scary designs that are fun, easy, and very safe.

Whatever creature or character you choose, it's important to have a dress rehearsal. Experiment so you can see what works, what's comfortable for your child, and what you'll need to change. Once you've achieved the perfect made-up face, pat on some baby powder as a finishing touch. It will help minimize smearing.

Getting Started

Sit down and plan out your strategy with your child. You'll want to be sure that he's comfortable with the process and is happy to have the various ingredients you suggest applied to his face.

Prepare your child's face by washing it with warm, soapy water and then drying it. If your child has oily skin, rubbing a little witch hazel on it with a cotton ball will help the makeup stay on better.

If necessary, tie or clip your child's hair back so that it's out of the way while you work.

Seat your child on a high stool near a table where you can spread out all your ingredients and tools. Wrap a towel or sheet around her shoulders so the rest of her stays clean.

Safety Tips

Treat eyes with care. Never put anything into or too close to your child's eyes such as drops of food coloring or even eyeliner. They can cause irritation or infections.

Test any product on the inside of your child's wrist or neck a day or two before using it on the face to make sure it doesn't cause an allergic reaction.

Never use paint on your child's skin. Use only non-toxic, washable products and cosmetics.

Safe adhesives are white school glue and corn syrup. Never use plastic cement, rubber cement, or instant contact glues on or near skin.

Special Effects

1 For scars and other creepy skin things, combine equal parts of unflavored gelatin and hot water, stir until gelatin dissolves. Let cool. As the mixture reaches room temperature it gets gooey enough to spread on your child's face. Mold it into a scar or simply cover the forehead, cheeks, nose, and chin in globs to create a truly icky effect.

2 You can add liquid makeup to the water before adding the gelatin to produce a natural skin tone. Or add a few drops of red food coloring to make a ghastly gash. (Caution: red dyes, food coloring, or makeup—even those that come with kits—can stain skin and clothing, so be careful. Use baby shampoo to wash it out.)

3 White school glue produces wonderful wrinkles and bumps. Simply stretch out the skin a bit with your hands and apply a thin layer of glue. Have your child blow it dry with a handheld hair dryer set on the lowest temperature while you hold and gently stretch the skin. When you let go, voilà—instant wrinkles. Work a small area at a time until the face is covered.

4 Or for a really monstrous skin condition, dampen some cereal flakes in a bowl and use white glue to stick it to your child's face. Yuck!

Witch

1 Use the flour and water mixture described in Ghoulish Hair to create a matted witch's 'do.

2 Use dots of green and white makeup, blended together with your fingertips to make a fiendishly, frightening skin tone.

3 Add some moles or warts by gluing pieces of puffed wheat cereal on to your child's nose or cheek.

4 Black out a tooth or two by drying it first with a tissue and then drawing on it with black or brown eyebrow pencil (which will wear off after a while) or look for tooth black at novelty or drug stores.

Fairy Princess

1 If your child has pale skin, use a light base to cover her face and neck. Apply a little blue eye shadow to her eyelids and pink to the bone just under the brow. Choose a pink blush and lipstick that are shiny and sparkly.

2 If your child has dark skin, select a darker foundation and stronger colors.

3 Finish off by spraying some sparkles in her hair (available in novelty and drug stores).

Vampire

1 Slick your child's hair back with hair gel or shampoo. Use a very pale foundation to cover the whole face right up to the hairline and including the neck and ears. Draw a widow's peak at the center of the hairline with an eyeliner pencil.

2 Apply dark brown or gray eye shadow around the eye sockets for a sunken effect. Add a touch of maroon-tinted lipstick to the lips.

3 Finish it off with store-bought plastic fangs.

Ghoulish Hair

1 To make hair stick out wildly in all directions, wet hair, towel dry, and apply shampoo (be careful not to work it into a lather). Mold the hair into the design you want and let it dry with the soap in. It will stay quite stiff until you rinse it out.

2 For even yuckier hair, mix up a paste of flour and water and work through child's hair. You can mat it down or mold into any design. Add some green food coloring and you'll have a wonderfully horrible hairdo.

Lion

1 Cover your child's whole face with a base of light orange makeup.

2 Apply white patches with a flat paintbrush above the eyebrows, on cheekbones, beneath nose, and on chin.

3 Then, using a small, stiff paintbrush and black or brown makeup or an eyebrow pencil, fill in eyebrows.

4 Draw one long dark stripe down the forehead with several others branching off from it. Draw a dark wavy line under each eye and another outlining the lower cheek.

5 Blacken the tip of the nose and the small indentation underneath it. Then outline chin and draw whiskers beside nose.

CHAPTER THREE

Pumpkins, Etc.

I remember, as a child, watching my mother carve our Halloween pumpkin. It was a struggle to cut out the small triangular features with an unwieldy kitchen knife. We didn't always manage to get the teeth going in the right direction and some of these jack-o'-lanterns were decidedly more successful than others.

Thankfully, there are now clever tool kits on the market created especially for carving pumpkins. With these tools to the rescue, carving pumpkins is easier than ever before and, therefore, the designs can be as amusing or enchanting as you wish to make them. Choose our Funny Face, swirling Autumn Leaves, or a Galaxy of Stars. You can mix and match our pattern shapes or create some of your own; cookie cutters and coloring books are good sources for inspiration.

But don't stop there! Pumpkins—and many fall veggies—can be decorated in a variety of other ways as well. For example, raid the attic and dress up a Pumpkin Head Family, or paint ghostly figures on butternut squash. You can even turn a pumpkin into a jewellike glittering centerpiece for a sophisticated celebration.

Although any actual cutting should be left for the adults, there are plenty of opportunities for children of all ages to participate. Going to the pumpkin patch to pick your own pumpkins is a great beginning.

Bet you can't make just one!

You Will Need

Pumpkin

Package of pumpkin-carving tools

Flat-edged ice-cream scoop or scraper scoop

Paring knife

Masking tape

Ballpoint pen

Pushpins, corsage pins, or straight pins

Petroleum jelly

Candle

Tracing paper or tissue paper

Pencil

Scissors

What to Do

1 Choose a pumpkin that is an appropriate size and shape for the design you wish to carve. Tall pumpkins may lend themselves better to faces. Large, round pumpkins with smooth surfaces work well for designs with lots of cutouts. Look for a pumpkin with a flat bottom that will sit upright.

2 Wipe the pumpkin clean with a soft damp cloth and dry.

3 Decide which patterns you want to use, and trace the design, actual size—or enlarge or reduce it on a photocopier—onto tracing paper.

4 *For a lid:* Draw a 6-sided lid with a V-shape notch at the back. This notch will serve as a guide to replace the lid. *For a bottom:* Draw an opening on the bottom of your pumpkin if you want to sit it over a candle. Be sure to draw the opening large enough so that it will be easy to reach inside and scoop out the contents when cut.

Carved Pumpkins

For this Funny Face pumpkin (left and page 54) cut two ear shapes (one from each side); then when you have completed the rest of the carving, put the tab inserts into the cutout holes and secure with straight pins. A little experience and a steady hand are required for the areas around the eyes. If in doubt, eliminate the teardrop shape directly under the eye to avoid carving the thinner strips. Pumpkins can be scooped out from the top or the bottom. Cut a lid or a bottom candle opening as desired.

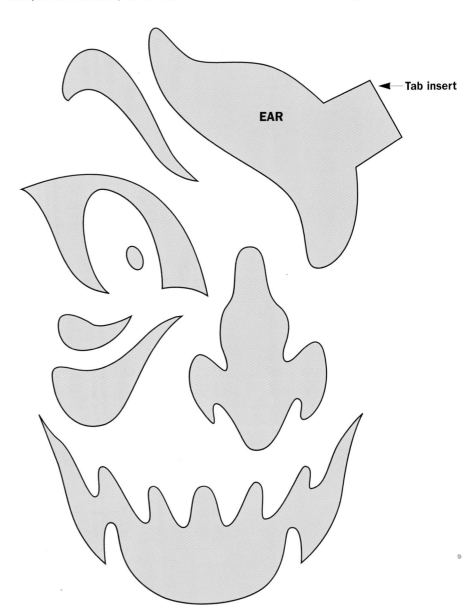

EAR

◄— **Tab insert**

L et the stars shine through, and a crescent moon as well, in this Galaxy of Stars design. Cut as many stars as fit your pumpkin and place the carved lantern on the doorstep or in a window to welcome trick-or-treaters.

5 Only grownups should do the actual cutting. To do so, cut along the drawn lines for the lid or bottom opening with a sharp paring knife. Keep your noncarving hand away from the blade at all times. If cutting a lid, angle the blade toward the center of the pumpkin to create a ledge that supports the lid. If cutting a bottom, cut straight into the pumpkin.

6 Scoop out the seeds and strings from inside the pumpkin—a good step for kids. Use a large spoon or ice-cream scoop or the plastic scraper scoop that is made for this purpose.

7 Scrape the inner pulp away from the area of the pumpkin that you plan to carve until the pumpkin wall is approximately 1 inch (2.5cm) thick. To check the thickness, insert a straight pin into the wall.

8 Tape the patterns to the pumpkin: It may be necessary to cut slashes in the edges of the paper for the patterns to fit smoothly in place.

9 To transfer the patterns to the pumpkin, use a pushpin, corsage pin, or the tip of the poker tool to poke holes through the paper and into the pumpkin along the design lines about $1/16$ inch (2mm) to $1/8$ inch (3mm) apart. Make sure that all of the lines have been transferred. Remove paper, and use a pen or dull-point pencil to connect the dots. Save the paper patterns to refer to while carving.

10 Cradle the pumpkin in your lap, and keep the pumpkin saw or small paring knife at a 90-degree angle to the pumpkin while carving. Carve from dot to dot to cut out the pattern shapes; if using the saw, don't try to slice with it, but saw with a gentle up and down motion *not* back and forth. It is definitely easier to create smaller and rounded shapes with the saw that is made for this purpose. If an

F alling leaves are the inspiration for this Autumn Leaves design. By scattering maple and elm leaf-shaped patterns at angles, the result is a windblown look that is appropriate for the season.

older child wants to help, the saw is much safer than a knife but still requires adult supervision. Do not exert too much pressure or the tools might break. Push the cut pieces into the pumpkin with your fingers. If a large piece becomes wedged, cut it into smaller pieces.

11 If you happen to cut through a pumpkin section by mistake, reattach the pieces with straight pins or toothpicks.

12 Rub all cut pumpkin edges with petroleum jelly to keep it fresh longer.

13 Insert a short column candle, votive or battery-operated light in the pumpkin. If the candle is not in a holder, form a holder from aluminum foil and secure the candle with a few drops of melted wax.

14 If candle smoke blackens the lid, cut a chimney hole in the lid top to vent the smoke and heat and preserve your design.

Going Batty describes the cutout designs circling all around this carved creation. Two different sizes fly over the surface. As with Autumn Leaves and Galaxy of Stars, this pumpkin looks equally enchanting from all sides. When not on display, store your carved pumpkin in a refrigerator with plastic wrap covering all the carved areas.

Pumpkin Head Family

These pumpkins have personality. A trip to the local flea market, rummage sale or simply your own attic will yield most of the supplies. Draw the expressions freehand or trace our patterns. Let each family member create his or her own Pumpkin Head or make this into a party game by providing the supplies and letting guests choose the "most original," "best likeness," or "wackiest ancestor." The prize? Why a pumpkin pie, of course.

You Will Need

Assorted pumpkins

Acrylic paints:
purple, green, black, white, and yellow

Small fine-tip paintbrushes

Old hats

Small nails or pushpins to hold hats in place

Black felt-tip marker

Pencil

Tracing paper

Masking tape

Optional: Yarn for hair and white glue for yarn hair

What to Do

1 For each pumpkin, choose features for eyes, nose, and mouth from the patterns given on page 62. Enlarge on a photocopier to desired size. Trace onto tracing paper.

2 Arrange traced features on the pumpkin and tape in place. Trace over the patterns again with a pencil to make a line impression on the pumpkin front.

3 Remove the paper and outline the shapes with the black marker.

4 Paint in the details as shown in the photo.

5 Glue on yarn for hair, if desired.

6 Add hats and pin or nail them securely in place so they won't fall off or blow away.

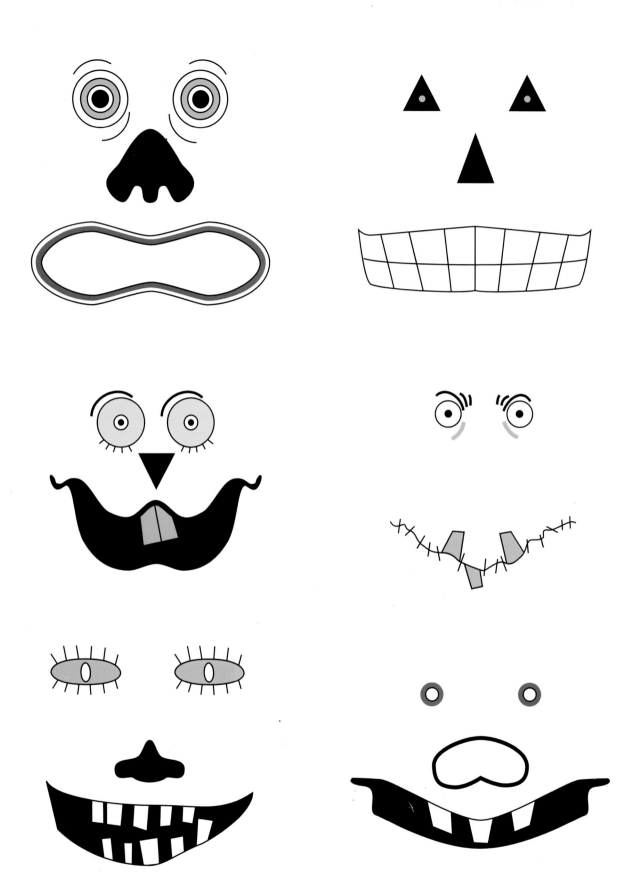

PUMPKIN HEAD FAMILY
Enlarge 200%

Father Hubbard

As the name states, this jaunty character is a hubbard squash wearing a painted face and a derby hat. The fun part of this project is finding yourself laughing aloud at the market while sorting through a pile of squash looking for face shapes. Some may actually remind you of someone you know.

You Will Need

Hubbard squash

Acrylic paint: black and white

Fine-tip paintbrush

Derby hat (or other man's hat)

Tracing paper

Pencil

Pushpins

Black marker

Masking tape

What to Do

1 Turn the squash so that the stem becomes the nose.

2 Try on the hat to approximate where you want to draw the features and mark where the bottom of hat covers the squash.

3 Trace the actual-size patterns for the mouth and 2 eyes onto tracing paper.

4 With a pushpin, prick holes in the tracing paper around all the pattern outlines. Cut paper features apart.

5 Tape the tracing paper pieces to the squash. With the marker, draw over the holes in the patterns to leave outlines of dots.

6 Remove the paper and connect the dots with the marker.

7 With a fine-tip paintbrush, outline all the black areas. Allow to dry. Then fill in with the white paint.

8 Secure the hat in place with pushpins.

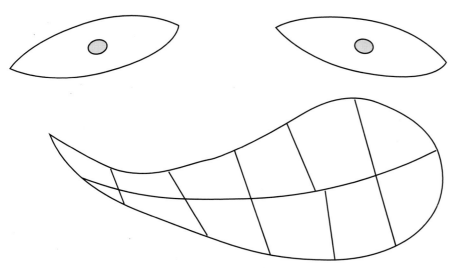

Cat Patrol

Guarding this windowsill is a Cat Patrol of acorn squash. All you need is some black paint, cardboard scraps, felt markers, and glitter glue. Children will love to make their own. You could also arrange them on a mantel or scatter them around the house in unexpected places—peering out of a cupboard, looking down from atop a bureau, behind a door, or even on a coat closet shelf.

You Will Need

Acorn squash in assorted sizes

Black acrylic paint

Medium-size paintbrush

Scraps of cardboard for ears, eyes, mouths, and whiskers

Glitter glue for whiskers and mouths

Colored markers: yellow, green, blue, and black

Tacky glue or a glue gun to attach ears, whiskers, etc.

Scissors

Pencil

Optional: Scraps of foil to line inside of ears (we used purple)

What to Do

1 Paint each squash black and allow to dry thoroughly. It may take 2 or 3 coats.

2 Turn the squash so the stem end becomes the nose.

3 From cardboard, draw and cut the following shapes for each: 2 elongated triangles for ears; 2 elliptical ovals for eyes; 2 small ovals for the center of each eye; optional small circles or strips to fit within the eye centers as shown in photo; 4 whiskers, approximately 3 inches (7.5cm) x ⅛ inch (3mm); an anchorlike shape for the mouth.

4 With markers, color ears black and other features blue, green, yellow, or black as desired.

5 Add glitter glue to the whiskers and mouths.

6 Optional: Cut 2 smaller triangles for each ear (to fit inside the first pair) from purple foil and glue in place.

7 Secure all features to the painted squash with tacky glue or a glue gun.

Ghastly Ghosts

Ghastly Ghosts are really butternut squash in disguise. Simply paint squash white and transfer one of the face patterns on pages 66-67 onto the squash and color between the lines with black paint. If the spirit moves you, paint initials or names on each one and use them as "place cards" at table settings and as take-home souvenirs.

You Will Need

Butternut squash

Acrylic paints: black and white

Medium-size paintbrush
for painting the squash

Fine-tip paintbrush,
for the faces

Pencil

Black felt-tip marker

Tracing paper

Masking tape

What to Do

1 Paint each squash with white paint. It will take 2 or 3 coats. Dry thoroughly between each coat.

2 Trace the pattern for the face of your choice onto tracing paper. If necessary, depending on the size of the squash, enlarge the pattern first on a photocopier.

3 Tape the tracing paper to the squash. Trace over the outlines with pencil to make a line impression. Remove the paper and outline the shapes with a black marker.

4 With black paint and the fine-tip brush, fill in all the shapes.

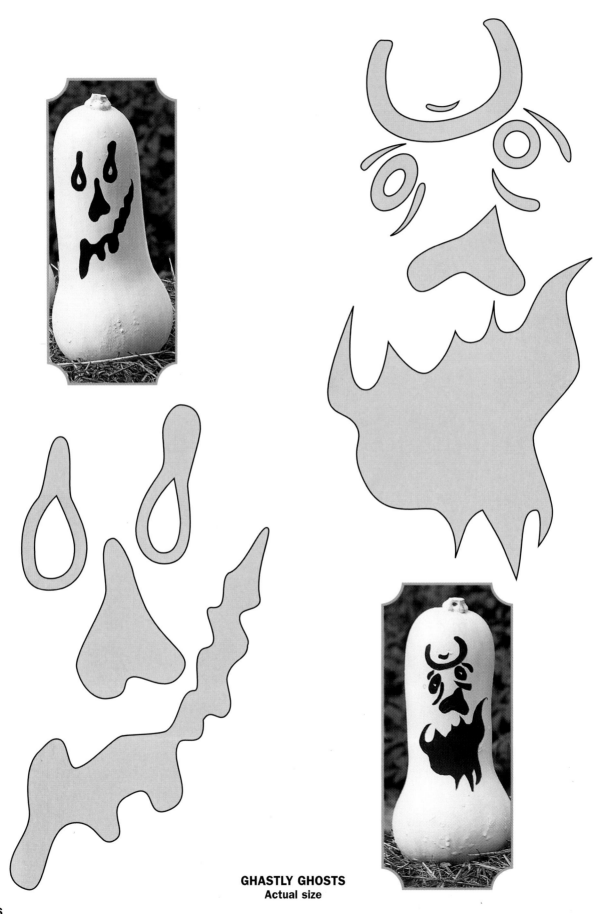

GHASTLY GHOSTS
Actual size

Sparkling Gems

Add a touch of glamour to the festivities with Cinderella-style pumpkins. These Sparkling Gems are a cinch to make. Just metallic spray paint and foil confetti provide the sparkle. It's best to display them on a sheltered porch or as an indoor centerpiece, as rain could wash away the glitter. Place several pumpkins by the front door for a magical entrance on a moonlit evening.

You Will Need

Well-shaped round pumpkin that stands straight

Gold and/or silver metallic spray paint

1 package of foil confetti

Spray adhesive

What to Do

1 Wipe the pumpkin carefully with a soft, damp cloth (or paper towel) and dry.

2 Spray-paint the entire pumpkin, including the stem, with metallic paint. It's a good idea to do this outdoors and place newspapers under the pumpkin to protect the grass or driveway. Allow to dry and add a second coat of paint.

3 If any orange shows through on the bottom area, turn the pumpkin on its side and spray again. Dry thoroughly.

4 Stand the pumpkin upright and spray adhesive around the top, stem area, as shown. Immediately sprinkle foil confetti on the adhesive while it is still tacky.

Gorgeous Gourds

What better solution to light up the festivities than using gourds (or miniature pumpkins or carnival squash) as candleholders? The only step required is to cut a hole in the center for a candle. However, this step should be done only by adults. Set your Gorgeous Gourds on a foil-lined tray and add fresh-cut flowers, then place the arrangement on a coffee table or buffet table and wait for the compliments.

You Will Need

Assorted gourds, carnival squash, or miniature pumpkins

Pumpkin carving tools (a lid-cutter saw)

Sharp knife

Taper and votive candles

What to Do

1 Insert the knife into the center of the gourd near the stem. Be careful, as gourds are very hard. Wedge the knife back and forth a little until you have a slit of about an inch. Remove the knife.

2 Insert the lid-cutter saw and gently and patiently saw—with an up-and-down sawing motion, (don't try to slice)—a circle in the center of the gourd. Don't push too hard or the saw can break. If this happens, try to finish the work with a grapefruit knife or apple corer. When the ends of the circle meet, remove the section of the gourd.

3 Drizzle a few drops of candle wax in the hole and insert a taper or votive candle as shown.

CHAPTER FOUR

Festive Fashions

Many adults look forward to dressing up at Halloween—either in costume, for parties—or by adding a special accessory. Some people even wear their outfits to work that day.

Most of us want to join in the festivities. And we really enjoy decorative accessories that can be worn for a week or several months. So, we've designed a collection of fashions that you'll want to wear again and again.

For those who like to crochet, there's a terrific Chenille Vest stitched in autumn colors—with pumpkin and cat motifs—that can be worn through the fall season and beyond. Then there's an amusing Denim Jacket and a machine-appliquéd Entertaining Apron that's perfect for hostesses. A Trick-or-Treat Shirt is embellished with fabric shapes: Start with a sweatshirt, use our patterns to cut out the fabric designs, and simply iron in place.

We've found that these projects are equally popular with teenagers and grandmothers alike. Why not invite several generations of friends and family members to get together and each make something unique? This is a good way to share skills and ideas. Start your own tradition by wearing these outfits every Halloween year after year.

Chenille Vest

This handsome, crocheted Chenille Vest is one that you'll enjoy wearing in fall. You can wear it with a shirt and jeans for causal occasions or with a pretty blouse and skirt for parties.

You Will Need

Chenille yarn: 3½ oz skeins in the following amounts and colors:

9 (10) skeins forest green

2 skeins orange

1 skein each black, brown and bright green

5 pumpkin buttons

Crochet hook size F/5 (4.00mm) or size required to obtain gauge.

Gauge: 16 sc and 16 rows equals 4 inches (10cm) over sc with size F/5 hook.

(To save time, take the time to check gauge.)

Sizes: Finished chest (buttoned): 38 inches (96.5cm) for Small (S) and 40 inches (101.5cm) for Medium (M).

Stitch Definitions:

Front post dc (Fpdc): Yo, from front, insert hook from front to back and around next stitch post, so hook is positioned horizontally and finish dc.

Back post dc (Bpdc): Same as front post dc, except that hook begins at back and wraps around front.

Dec 1 sc: (Yo and pull up a loop in next st) twice, yo and through 3 loops on hook.

Inc 1 sc: Work 2 sc in same st.

Inc 2 sc: Ch 3, sc in 2nd ch from hook.

NOTE: These instructions use US terms and abbreviations (see page 139). For Canadian terms, see conversions on page 139.

What to Do

Back: With forest green, ch 82 (86).

Row 1: Sc in 2nd ch from hook and in each ch across — 81 (85) sc.

Row 2: Ch 1 (counts as first sc), sc in each sc across, turn. Rep row 2 until piece measures 10 inches (25.5cm) from beg.

Shape armholes: Next row: (Do not ch 1), sl st across first 2 sts, sc in each sc to end of row. Rep last row 5 times more — 69 (73) sc. Cont in sc, dec 1 sc at each armhole edge every other row 8 times — 53 (57) sc. Work even in sc until armholes measure 8 (8½) inches, 20.5 (21.5) cm.

Shape neck and shoulders: Next row: Ch 1, sc in each of next 8 (9) sc for first shoulder. Fasten off. Join forest green at 8 (9) sc from other armhole edge. **Next row:** Ch 1, sc in each of these 8 (9) sc for second shoulder. Fasten off.

Left Front: With forest green, ch 4. **Row 1:** Sc in 2nd ch from hook and in each ch across — 3 sc. Work in sc following chart and shaping point until row 17 has been completed — 38 (40) sc. Cont even in sc following chart until beg of armhole shaping.

Shape armhole and neck: Shape armhole as for back; *At the same time*, dec 1 st at neck edge every other row 16 (17) times — 8 (9) sc remain. Cont even in sc until arm-hole measures same as back to shoulder. Fasten off.

Right Front: Work as for Left Front, reversing shaping and pattern place-ment.

Finishing: Holding fronts and back with right sides tog, using yarn end, sc shoulders sts tog. Sc side seams tog.

Rib Edging: Rnd 1: From right side, join forest green at one shoulder seam, dc evenly around entire out-side edge of vest, working 3 sc in same sc at each front point and at beg of V-neck shaping and working dc in every other st around neck edge, end with sl st to beg dc. Mark for 5 buttonholes evenly spaced on Left Front of vest. **Rnd 2:** Ch 2 (counts as first dc), skip first st, *1 fpdc into next st, 1 bpdc into next st; rep from * working buttonholes oppo-site markers as follows: fpdc in next st, ch 2, skip next st, fpdc in next st, cont as est, ending with sl st to top of beg ch. **Rnd 3:** Work as for rnd 2, working a dc into each ch-2 space of rnd 2. Fasten off. Sew on buttons opposite buttonholes.

Armhole Ribbing: Rnd 1: From right side, join forest green at side seam, dc even around armhole, join with sl st to beg dc. **Rnd 2:** Rep rib edging rnd 2, omitting buttonholes. Fasten off.

Embroidery for Pumpkins: From right side, with brown, work 2 ch sts on each pumpkin stem. With bright green, work a tendril and a leaf with backstitches. With black, work cross-stitch features on pumpkin faces.

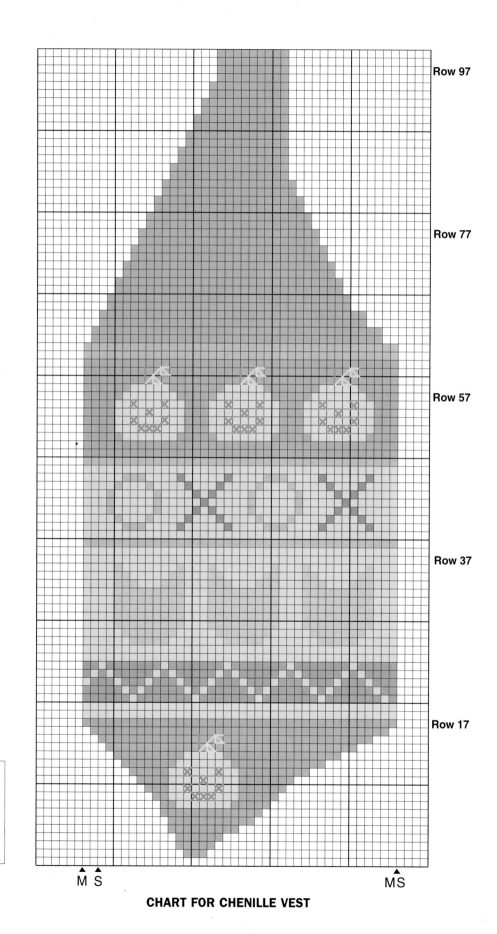

Row 97

Row 77

Row 57

Row 37

Row 17

▢ = Black
▢ = Brown
▢ = Orange
▢ = Forest Green
▢ = Bright Green

▲ ▲
M S

▲
M S

CHART FOR CHENILLE VEST

Entertaining Apron

Dress the part of hostess by machine-stitching a bat appliqué to the bib and adding pumpkin pockets to make this Entertaining Apron. Use a ready-made apron or follow our directions to make your own. (The same motifs could be applied to place mats.)

You Will Need

1 yard ticking stripe fabric for apron

¼ yard (.25m) orange pin-dot fabric for pumpkin appliqués

¼ yard (.25m) black fabric for bat, cats, and pumpkin face appliqués

Scraps of yellow (for mouth) and green (for stems) fabrics

Thread to match fabrics

White thread to embroider cat face, whiskers, and all eyes

Paper-backed fusible web

2 squares of tear-away stabilizer, 12 inches (30.5cm) each

Large sheet of paper for apron pattern

What to Do

Making the Apron:

1 Enlarge apron pattern on page 77 onto tracing paper, brown paper, or newspaper and cut apron from ticking fabric. (You may have to tape sections of paper together to fit.)

2 Cut 2 strips of ticking 3 by 29 inches (7.5 by 73.5cm) for ties and one strip of ticking 3 by 21 inches (7.5 by 53.5cm) for neck band.

3 Turn under ¼ inch (6mm) on all edges of apron and press. Turn under another ¼ inch (6mm) and stitch close to pressed edge.

4 To make the ties, fold the two long strips in half lengthwise with right sides together. Stitch with a ½ inch (1.3cm) seam allowance along one short edge and long edge. Turn right side out and press.

Entertaining Apron

5 To make neck band, fold remaining strip in half lengthwise with right sides together. Stitch along the long edge with a ½ inch (1.3cm) seam allowance, turn right side out and press.

6 Fold raw edge of ties under ½ inch (1.3cm) and press. Stitch ties to inside edge of sides of apron.

7 Turn under ½ inch (1.3cm) on ends of neck band and stitch band to inside of top apron front.

Note: You may want to try on apron to adjust neck band before sewing in place.

Making the Bat Appliqué:

8 Trace bat pattern on page 78 onto paper side of the fusible web.

9 Fuse web to the wrong side of black fabric. Cut out, remove paper, and fuse bat to apron bib.

10 By machine, satin-stitch around bat with black thread: stitches should enclose the edges of the appliqué.

11 Machine- or hand-embroider eyes.

Making the Pockets:

12 Enlarge pattern on page 78 for pumpkin/cat appliqué 150% to actual size as indicated.

13 Trace along outline indicated for orange shaded area *only* onto paper side of fusible web.

14 Next, trace and cut out each remaining section of the appliqué design (one cat plus eyes, nose, mouth, and stem for pumpkin) separately. Trace around these sections on the paper side of fusible web.

15 You may wish to label pieces by color: "green" for stem, "yellow" for mouth etc., then cut out.

16 Fuse each section to wrong side of appropriate color fabric and cut out. *Patterns are the reverse of the way they appear on finished apron.* Flop patterns to cut a mirror image of each piece for second pocket, as cats are facing each other.

17 Remove paper from each piece, one at a time, and fuse cat, pumpkin eyes, nose, mouth, and stem to orange shape. (See General Directions section on Machine Appliqué.)

18 By machine, satin-stitch around the edges of the pumpkin mouth, eyes, nose, base of stem, and cat. *Do not stitch around the outside of pumpkin yet.*

19 Pin assembled pumpkin/cat motif to tear-away stabilizer.

20 By machine, satin-stitch along the *top* edge of pumpkin, pumpkin stem, and cat *only* as shown in diagram below. Gently tear away stabilizer. Repeat for motif for second pocket.

21 Pin pumpkin pockets in place on apron front. Satin-stitch around the sides and base of each pumpkin.

22 Using a marking pencil or dressmaker's chalk, draw the cat's face, whiskers, and the pumpkin's eyes. Machine-stitch over marked lines with white thread, using a small zigzag stitch.

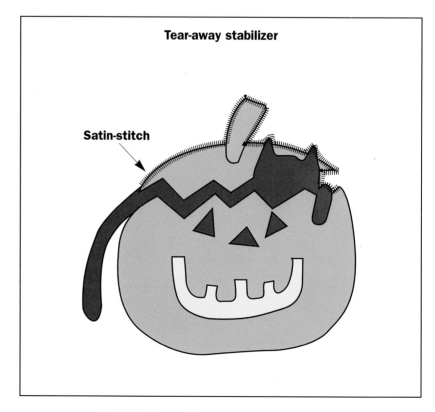

ASSEMBLY DIAGRAM FOR APRON POCKET
(Steps 19 and 20)

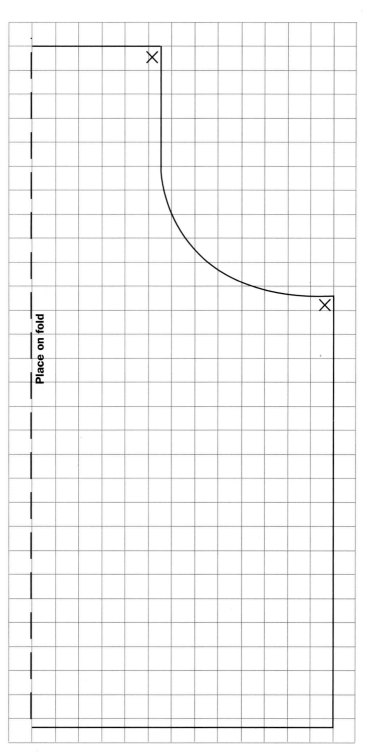

Place on fold

REDUCED PATTERN FOR ENTERTAINING APRON
Each square equals 1 inch (2.5cm).

Entertaining Apron

BAT PATTERN FOR ENTERTAINING APRON
Actual size
Use 70% for medium bat on Denim Jacket
50% for small bat on Denim Jacket

PUMPKIN/CAT PATTERN FOR
ENTERTAINING APRON & DENIM JACKET
Enlarge 150%

Denim Jacket

P eople will be talking (and smiling) behind your back when you wear this delightful Denim Jacket. Cut out our pattern designs, fuse them in place, and machine-appliqué around the edges.

of the way they will appear on the finished jacket.

5 Remove paper from each piece, one at a time, and fuse sections to center back of jacket, beginning with the orange pumpkin shape. Fit the cat and other pumpkin pieces in place. (See General Directions section on Machine Appliqué.)

Making the Bats and Stars:
6 Reduce bat pattern on page 78 70% for medium-size bat and 50% for small bats. Use patterns to draw 2 small bats and one medium-size bat onto paper side of fusible web.
7 Draw 10 freehand stars or use the patterns on page 57 or 81 on paper side of fusible web.
8 Fuse each pattern piece to the wrong side of the appropriate color fabric (purple for bats and yellow for stars) and cut out.

Appliquéing the Jacket:
9 Place bats and stars on jacket in desired locations around pumpkin/cat motif. Mark spots with pins, remove paper from each piece, one at a time, and fuse to jacket.
10 Set sewing machine to a satin stitch and stitch around the outer edge of each appliqué piece with matching thread. The stitching should enclose the edge of the fabric.
11 Using marking pen, draw cat's face and whiskers and bat and pumpkin eyes. Machine-stitch features using a narrow zigzag stitch and white thread.

You Will Need

¼ yard (.25m) orange pin-dot fabric for pumpkin

⅛ yard (.15m) purple fabric for bats

⅛ yard (.15m) yellow fabric for stars and pumpkin mouth

Small piece of black fabric for cat and pumpkin face

Scrap of green fabric for stem

Paper-backed fusible web

Pencil

Marking pen

Threads to match fabric

White thread to embroider cat face and whiskers and all eyes

Scissors

What to Do
Making the Pumpkin/Cat Appliqué:
1 Enlarge pattern for pumpkin/cat 150% as directed on page 78.
2 First trace along outline indicated for orange pumpkin shape only of pumpkin/cat appliqué, (see facing page,) onto paper side of fusible web.
3 Then trace and cut out remaining sections of the appliqué design (one cat plus eyes, nose, mouth, and stem for pumpkin) separately. Trace around these sections on the paper side of fusible web. You may wish to label pieces by color: "green" for stem, "yellow" on mouth etc., then cut out.
4 Fuse each section to the wrong side of the appropriate color fabric and cut out. *Patterns are the reverse*

Trick-or-Treat Shirt

This sweatshirt turned cardigan is certain to be one of your most comfortable "costumes" this season. All the motifs on our Trick-or-Treat Shirt are cut from small-print cotton fabrics and ironed in place with fusible web.

You Will Need

Gray sweatshirt

9 dark gray buttons, $^3/_4$-inch (2cm)

$^3/_4$ yard (.70m) paper-backed heavy-duty fusible web

Small print cotton fabrics in the following amounts:

$^1/_8$ yard (.15m) brown, for fence

$^1/_4$ yard (.25m) sturdy gray brick pattern, for button plackets

12 x 12 inches (30.5 x 30.5cm) black, for cat and blocks

12 x 6 inches (30.5 x 15cm) orange, for pumpkins

4 x 6 inches (10 x 15cm) green, for leaves

4 x 4 inches (10 x 10cm) light brown, for stems

3 x 3 inches (7.5 x 7.5cm) mustard, for moon

5 x 6 inches (12.5 x 15cm) light gray, for stars

6 x 6 inches (15 x 15cm) muslin, for Trick-or-Treat blocks

Black fine-tip permanent marking pen

Yardstick

Tracing paper and pencil

Scissors and pinking shears

What to Do

1 Prewash sweatshirt and appliqué fabrics to remove any sizing. Press with warm iron to remove wrinkles.
2 With a ruler and pencil, mark a line on center front of sweatshirt from neck edge to bottom edge. Cut along this line.

Making the Front Placket:

3 To make front placket, cut 2 strips of sturdy gray patterned fabric 3 inches (7.5cm) wide and 2 inches (5cm) longer than the length of the shirt.

4 Fold one strip in half lengthwise, right side in. Press on fold. Turn each long edge of strip $^1/_4$ inch (6mm) to wrong side for seam allowances, and press.
5 Turn strip right side up and place over one cut edge of shirt front, with seam allowances folded in and 1 inch (2.5cm) extending at top and bottom of sweatshirt.
6 Fold strip where it extends at top and bottom to wrong side, and pin. Baste strip in place and remove

pins. From front of shirt, topstitch through all layers, over the basting seam. Remove basting stitches.

7 Repeat with remaining strip on other side of shirt. Stitch buttons, evenly spaced, to left placket. Make buttonholes on right placket to correspond.

Making the Motifs:

8 Cut fusible web to same size as fabrics and fuse to wrong side of each color fabric. Enlarge designs as directed, trace onto paper-backed side of fusible web, and cut out as follows: one black cat; 3 orange pumpkins, one each size; 6 green leaves; 3 light brown stems; and 4 light gray stars. *Patterns are the reverse of the way they appear on the front of the shirt.*

9 Draw and cut out one freehand circle 2½-inches (6.5cm) in diameter for moon from mustard; for fence, cut 12 strips 1-inch (2.5cm) wide and ranging in length from 9 to 11 inches (23 to 28cm) from dark brown; cut points at one end of 8 of the strips.

10 Cut out patterns, remove paper backing as you use them, and fuse in place as shown in photo. Begin with 4 vertical fence posts of varying heights on each side, pointed ends up, and spaced about 1 inch (2.5cm) apart. Then add 2 horizontal fence posts on each side, angled, about 3 inches (7.5cm) apart.

11 Next add pumpkins, inserting each stem before fusing: from left to right, large, small, and medium. Add 2 leaves to each pumpkin.

12 Position cat on fence and fuse in place. With fine-tip marking pen, draw on whiskers.

13 For Trick-or-Treat blocks, use pinking shears to cut 2 slightly irregular rectangles approximately 2 x 3 inches (5 x 7.5cm) and one square

2½ x 2½ inches (6.5 x 6.5cm) from black. With regular scissors, cut 3 muslin blocks ¼ inch (6mm) smaller on all sides than black blocks. Using black fine-tip permanent marker, letter "Trick-or-Treat" words on each block, using the smallest one for

"or." Fuse muslin blocks to right side of black blocks. Peel paper backing off black fabric and fuse to left of shirt front as shown in photo.

14 Finish by adding moon and 2 stars above cat and 2 stars on left between lettered blocks.

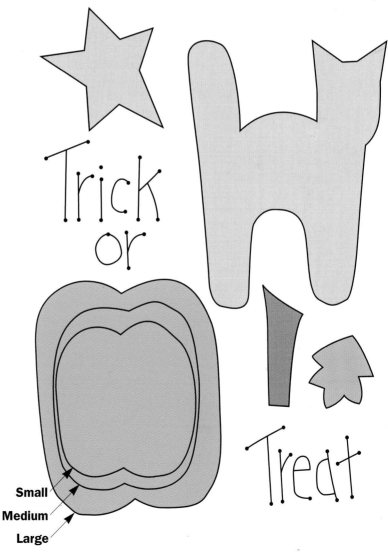

Small
Medium
Large

REDUCED PATTERNS FOR TRICK-OR-TREAT SHIRT
Enlarge 200%.

CHAPTER FIVE

Fun Foods

Halloween is one of the best holidays for cooks who don't want to spend a lot of time in the kitchen. There are no five-course formal dinners to cook and serve. Get-togethers are casual and finger foods are often called for. It's not so much what you prepare as how you present it. And to make it easy on yourself, take advantage of the wonderful baking and decorating supplies such as cookie cutters, bread and cake tins, and molds that are available for this particular holiday.

For example, we chose cookie cutters that spell out "BOO" and "EEK" as well as ghost shapes for our cookies. You can also use these cutters to make special lunchbox sandwiches—just cut shapes from bread and add peanut butter. Mini-pumpkin pans can be used to make individual brown bread treats and to bake sandwich buns for hors d'oeuvres, and cat and bat molds can be used for gelatin desserts. For family only—or brunch for friends—the jack-o'-lantern pancakes are sure to delight!

All of these designs and recipes are the creations of Wilton Enterprises' food expert and master cake decorator, Zella Junkin. My favorite is Zella's clever Frightful Sweets. All you need are packaged snack cakes, tubes of icing, and ready-made decorations to make the Mummy and the Witch. Decorate the cakes in advance to wow your guests or have enough supplies on hand for everyone to participate and join in the fun.

Halloween Cookies

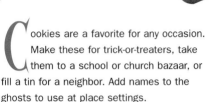

C ookies are a favorite for any occasion. Make these for trick-or-treaters, take them to a school or church bazaar, or fill a tin for a neighbor. Add names to the ghosts to use at place settings.

You Will Need

Halloween cookie cutters: BOO, EEK, and ghost shapes

Tube of black icing gel, to outline BOO and EEK cookies and add features to ghosts

Orange and black paste food colors to color dough

Royal Icing for ghost cookies, see recipe, Step 11

Pastry brush

1 cup (2 sticks) butter (250g), softened

1 cup (200g) sugar

1 large egg

1 teaspoon vanilla

2 teaspoons baking powder

3 cups (375g) all-purpose flour

Egg yolk for solid orange cookies

What to Do

1 Preheat oven to 400°F.

2 In large bowl, cream butter and sugar with an electric mixer. Beat in egg and vanilla.

3 Add baking powder and then flour one cup at a time, mixing after each addition. The dough will be very stiff, blend last flour in by hand. (If necessary add a little water to dough if crumbly.) Do not chill dough.

4 Divide dough into three balls. Set one aside and leave uncolored. Knead or mix orange food color in the second ball and black food color into the third. Cover each ball with plastic wrap and keep covered when not working with it.

5 For all cookies, roll dough slightly thinner than the cutter.

6 To make uncolored cookies, roll dough and cut various shapes.

7 To make striped cookies roll sections of colored and uncolored dough together, side by side, and then cut out cookies.

8 For the orange BOO and EEK cookies, in the foreground, use uncolored dough. After cutting out shapes, mix orange food color with egg yolk and "paint" cookies with pastry brush before baking.

9 Place cookies on ungreased cookie sheet and bake 15-20 minutes or until

lightly browned. Cool 5 minutes, then remove and cool completely on a rack.

Recipe makes 3-4 dozen cookies.

Icing the Cookies

10 To decorate BOO and EEK cookies, outline baked cookies with black icing gel as shown in photo.

11 For ghost cookies, leave uncolored and add features with black icing gel or color white with Royal Icing made as follows:

3 egg whites,

1 pound confectioners' sugar,

1/2 teaspoon cream of tartar.

Beat all ingredients at high speed for 7 to 10 minutes or until icing forms stiff peaks. To thin, add 3 to 4 tablespoons water, a small amount at a time until icing is the consistency of heavy cream. "Paint" icing on ghost shapes with a pastry brush.

Recipe will ice 2 dozen cookies.

Mini Pumpkin Sandwiches

Sure to be a crowd-pleaser at parties, these mini-buns perk up any sandwich fillings. An easy-to-serve (and eat) finger food idea. Children will enjoy bite-size burgers.

What to Do

1 Thaw frozen bread dough or prepare hot roll mix according to package directions.

2 Preheat oven to 350°F. Spray petite pumpkin pan with vegetable cooking spray.

3 Roll dough with floured hands into ¾ inch (2cm) diameter balls.

4 Press balls firmly into pan cavities and into face indentations in each cavity; let rise following package directions. (Place remaining dough in the refrigerator until ready to bake.)

5 Bake 15-20 minutes or until edges are browned.

6 Cool; remove breads from pan.

7 Pumpkin buns are small and will dry out quickly. Keep well covered with a damp cloth or plastic wrap until ready to serve.

8 Split buns and fill with cold cuts and lettuce. Serve with condiments.

Recipe makes 16-18 sandwiches.

You Will Need

12-cavity Petite Pumpkin pan

One 16-ounce (500g) loaf frozen bread dough or one package hot roll mix

Vegetable cooking spray

2 pounds (1 kg) favorite cold cuts

Lettuce

Mustard or other condiments

Brown Bread Pumpkins

You Will Need

12-cavity Petite Pumpkin pan

Pastry bag with #2 or #3 round tip

Orange paste food color,
for cream cheese

Vegetable cooking spray, to coat pan

¾ cup (85g) whole wheat flour

2 tablespoons graham-cracker crumbs

⅓ cup (40g) all-purpose flour

¼ cup (35g) cornmeal

1 teaspoon baking soda

1 teaspoon pumpkin pie spice

1 cup (250ml) buttermilk

¼ cup (60ml) molasses

3 ounces (90g) cream cheese, softened

Optional: ½ cup (70g) raisins

What to Do

1 Preheat oven to 350°F. Spray pumpkin pan with vegetable cooking spray.
2 In large bowl, mix dry ingredients together. Stir buttermilk and molasses together and add to dry ingredients. Stir until smooth. Add raisins, if desired.
3 Spoon batter into pan cavities until full. Bake 15-20 minutes or until a toothpick inserted in center comes out clean. Cool 5 minutes; remove.
4 Tint cream cheese with orange food color. Using a pastry bag and round tip #2 or #3, add facial features as shown in photo.
5 Serve at room temperature with baked beans, stew, or soup.

Recipe makes 3 dozen.

These decorative treats are a wonderful change of pace to accompany any course. For example, serve with stew or soup (pumpkin, of course) ladled into a small hollowed-out pumpkin or squash.

Shimmering Bat and Cat

You Will Need

Bat and cat pans/molds (1-cup [250ml] cavity)

Black paste food color

Candies (for eyes)

One 3-ounce (90g) package grape gelatin dessert mix

1 cup (250ml) grape juice

Whipped cream

Optional: Sprinkles or colored sugar for whipped cream

What to Do

1 Make gelatin according to package directions, substituting grape juice for cold water.
2 Add food color until gelatin is black.
3 Rinse bat and cat pans with cold water, pour in gelatin. Refrigerate for 4 hours or until firm.
4 Unmold by dipping 5-10 seconds in warm water.

5 Add candy for eyes.
6 Serve with whipped cream garnished with sprinkles or with colored sugar, if desired.

Recipe makes 4 molds

As a side dish or a dessert, quivering bats and cats colored black will steal the show. These same pans can be used for individual cakes as well.

Jack-o'-Lantern Pancakes

You Will Need

jack-o'-lantern-shaped pan
12 x 11 inches (30.5 x 27.9cm)

2 cups (250g) biscuit mix

2 tablespoons packed light brown sugar

2 teaspoons ground cinnamon

1½ cups (12 ounce [375ml] can)
undiluted evaporated milk
or evaporated skim milk

½ cup (125g) solid-pack pumpkin

Vegetable oil

2 large eggs

½ stick (125g) butter, for face

Honey or syrup

What to Do

1 Preheat oven to 450°F. Place empty jack-o'-lantern pan in oven.
2 In large bowl, combine biscuit mix, sugar, cinnamon, evaporated milk, pumpkin, 2 tablespoons vegetable oil, and eggs. Beat or whisk until smooth. (Batter may be stored overnight in refrigerator. Stir before using.)
3 When oven is preheated, remove pan. CAUTION: Pan will be very hot. Coat pan lightly with a couple of drops of vegetable oil or a small amount of butter and rotate pan to cover evenly. Pour 2 cups of batter in pan. Pour in a circle to cover pan evenly. Push to edges if necessary.
4 Return to oven and bake 6-8 minutes or until top is dry and edges are brown. Top will not be brown.
5 Invert baked pancake onto serving dish.
6 Repeat for next pancake. You can place finished pancake on a cookie sheet and return to oven for the last 2 minutes of cooking time to reheat.
7 Garnish pancakes with butter or margarine features: Cut butter or margarine into ⅛-inch (3mm) slices and then halve for triangles for eyes and halve again into smaller triangles for mouth as shown in photo. Serve with honey or syrup.

Recipe makes 2 pancakes; each pancake serves 2.

Pancakes can be enjoyed any time of day. Have butter triangles, raisins, or nuts available and let children (or adults) add their own funny faces. To feed a crowd, buy two or three pans so that you can make several pancakes at the same time.

Frightful Sweets

You Will Need

For the Witch

Packaged cream-filled snack cakes

Tube of green icing, for hair

Tube of black icing, for hat and arms

#104 petal tip, for hat brim

#10 large round tip, for hat and arms

#233 multiple-opening tip, for hair

#3 round tip, for nose

Coupler ring set, to fit tips to tubes

Tube of black decorating gel, for eyes

Tube of red decorating gel, for mouth

Ready-made jack-o'-lantern icing decorations

For the Mummy

Packaged cream-filled snack cakes

Tube white icing, for bandage strips

#104 flat tip, for icing strips

Tube of black decorating gel, for eyes

Coupler ring set, to fit tip to tube

Ready-made bat icing decorations

What to Do

1 Unwrap cakes and place on small serving plates.
2 Use coupler ring to attach tips to tubes of icing.

For the Witch

3 With tip #233 and green icing, pipe hair by squeezing out icing on cake (as shown in photo), then pulling out to make hair. Stop squeezing tube before pulling the tip away.
4 To make pointed hat, use the black icing and tip #10. Squeeze out a large dot and then pull tip out for hat. Use the same tip to pipe strips on each side for arms. For the brim of the hat, use black icing and tip #104 and pipe a strip around the hat for the brim.

5 With black gel, pipe dots for eyes. With red gel, pipe a strip for the mouth. With green icing and #10 tip, squeeze a dot for nose and pull tip away to extend dot upright.
6 Add jack-o'-lantern icing decoration between arms as shown.

Recipe decorates 6 witches.

For the Mummy

7 With white icing and #104 tip, pipe strips for bandages all around cake as shown in photo, leaving space for eyes.
8 With black gel, pipe dots for eyes.
9 Add bat icing decoration as shown.

Recipe decorates 6 mummies.

Even if you have never tried your hand at cake decorating before, you can still decorate these snack cakes. Just squeeze tubed icing through metal or plastic tips. The only trick is not to eat them as fast as you make them. However, if you do make a mistake, it's easy to destroy the evidence.

CHAPTER SIX

Toys and Gifts

This is the time of year to fantasize about ghouls, goblins, and things that go "boo" in the night. Make-believe creatures stand watch on a flight of stairs, peer down from a ceiling beam, and perch on a mantel or office shelf.

We've designed a bevy of beasties that are adorable, rather than scary. These are the kind of toys that children will hug tightly during the reading of a ghost story and then want tucked into bed beside them.

The "Haunted" Doll House is a wonderful project that the whole family can make together—it's one that you won't want to put away after the holiday. And kids and cat lovers alike will find the Scaredy Cats Quilt eerily irresistible.

Our Cool Cats can double as pillows on a sofa and the easy-to-make My Three Witches (or four or five) can either be lined up on a windowsill or given as fabulous party favors. That's why many of the ideas in this chapter are also appealing as gifts for adults.

"Haunted" Doll House

To make a "Haunted" Doll House for your own family of ghosts, all it takes is sheets of Styrofoam®, white glue, and paint. Furnishings are made from recycled containers, corks, lids, and fabric scraps.

You Will Need
to build house

6 sheets of Styrofoam® brand plastic foam 18 x 12 x 1-inch (46 x 30.5 x 2.5cm)

Craft knife with sharp blades

T-square

Tacky white glue

Gray or tan acrylic paint, for house

Green acrylic paint for roof

Paintbrush

Pencil

What to Do

Cutting the House Pieces:

1 Number the Styrofoam sheets and cut as follows: From sheet #1, one 18 x 9-inch (45 x 23cm) piece for front of house. From sheet #2, one 18 x 9-inch (45 x 23cm) piece for left side of house. From sheet #3, one 18 x 9-inch (45 x 23cm) piece for right side of house. From sheet #4, two 9 x 8-inch (23 x 20.5cm) pieces for interior floors. From sheet #5, one 9 x 8-inch (23 x 20.5cm) piece for interior floor and one triangular piece that has an 11-inch (27.9cm) base and is 5¼-inches (13.3cm) high, for peaked front of house. From sheet #6, one piece 12 x 9 inches (30.5 x 23cm) and another 12 x 8 inches (30.5 x 20.5cm) for 2 halves of roof.

2 From remaining Styrofoam scraps, cut the following pieces: one 8 x 3-inch (20.5 x 7.5cm) for porch floor; one 9 x 3-inch (23 x 7.5cm) for porch roof; two 4½ x 1-inch (11.5 x 2.5cm) for porch pillars; one 2½ x ¾ x ½-inch (6.5 x 2 x 1.3cm) for step; four 8 x ⅜ x ⅜-inch (20.5 x 1 x 1cm) for supports for interior floors.

Cutting Out Windows and Doors:

3 On one side piece center, measure and mark a window 3½-inches square (9cm) and 3 inches (7.5cm) from the bottom. Mark a same-size window for second floor, 4½ inches (11.5cm) above the top of the first floor window. Cut out windows. Repeat on remaining side piece.

4 For front of house, center one window measuring 2½-inches (6.5cm) square on the triangular peak piece. This window is placed ½-inch (1.3cm) above the 11-inch (28cm) side of the triangle.

5 Center the door and the second floor window on the front piece. The door measures 3½ x 4½ inches (9 x 11.5cm) and is placed 1 inch (2.5cm) above bottom edge of foam sheet. The window measures 3½-inches square (9cm) and is placed 4½ inches (11.5cm) above the top of the door.

Assembling the House:

6 With white glue, glue the sides to the front so that the house measures 11 inches (28cm) across. Glue the first floor inside house. Glue peak onto top of front piece. Let dry.

7 Glue second floor into the house 6¼ inches (15.8cm) above top edge of first floor. Glue third floor into the house with bottom 6¼ inches (15.8cm) above top edge of the second floor. Glue foam strips into back corners under each floor for supports.

8 Glue front porch floor to center of house. Glue one pillar to the right of porch. Glue porch roof onto front of house at a slight angle and rest it on top of the pillar.

9 Use a sharp pencil to make cracks and to gouge holes into exteriors of house and roof pieces. Paint house gray or tan. Break the second pillar in half and paint to match. Allow everything to dry. Glue broken pillar in place to left of front door, as shown in photo.
10 Paint roof pieces green on all surfaces. When dry, glue the 8-inch (20.5cm) roof piece to left front of peak. Glue the 9-inch (23cm) roof piece to the right side of peak: it will overlap the left one. Let dry.

You Will Need
to decorate the outside

Sphagnum and/or Spanish moss

Acrylic stretch spider web

Craft sticks, and/or tongue depressors, for windows and doors

Clear plastic, for window panes (recycled food containers were used here)

Small jar brown acrylic paint and brush

Black fine-point permanent marker

Red permanent marker

Tacky white glue

Craft knife

What to Do

11 Cut clear plastic to fit windows. Cut jagged holes for cracks and "broken" windows with craft knife. Glue windows in place.
12 Use craft knife to cut craft sticks to "board up" windows and door. (It's best for an adult to do the cutting.) Stain the sticks with 30% water-diluted brown acrylic paint. Use black marker to make little dots to represent nails at the end of each stick. Glue sticks over windows and door. Letter "Keep Out" with red marker and add "13" to the pillar with black marker.

13 Glue bits of moss onto house and around the base. Drape acrylic spider web around house. (We also added a few newspaper scraps at front door.)

You Will Need
to decorate the interior

Colorful felt for wall-to-wall carpet

Scraps of fabric for curtains, bedspreads, tablecloths

Recycled objects such as corks, bottle caps, spools, small jewelry boxes, plastic lids, milk and fruit-juice container tops, cardboard paper tubes, etc. to make furniture.

Small jar acrylic paint as desired, for chairs or other details

Tacky white glue

What to Do

14 Cut and glue felt to floors for carpeting. Cut and glue fabric to windows for curtains.
15 To make a table (see one on ground floor), glue a plastic coffee can lid on top of a large spool. Our table has 3 upright bottle caps for plates and the centerpiece is a wooden bead with tiny artificial flowers in it.
16 To make stools, glue milk or fruit-juice container tops onto corks. To make chairs, use the top of a spray can for seat. For back, cut a section of cardboard tubing or file folder paper. Paint top and back to match and glue together.
17 To make beds, glue 4 small thread spools to bottom of a plastic foam rectangle. Cover bed with fabrics. Use a small piece of cotton or polyfill batting for pillow.
18 Use small jewelry boxes to make tables, then drape with fabric.
19 Make a lamp by gluing a wooden skewer into a large, flat wooden bead for base (or a scrap of foam). Glue an inverted creamer cup to the top of the skewer as a lamp shade.

Glue lace around the edge and a bead to the top of the creamer.

You Will Need
to make a ghost family

3 small Styrofoam® brand plastic foam cones, 3- to 4-inches (7.5 to 10cm) high, for ghost bodies

Three 1-inch (2.5cm) Styrofoam® brand plastic foam balls, for ghost heads

White pipe cleaners, for arms

Scraps of white felt to drape over arms

Black permanent marker, for faces

Craft knife

Tacky white glue

Scissors

Optional: white paint for body and head

What to Do

20 With the craft knife, cut the tips off the cones. Glue a ball onto the top of each cone for a head. Paint cone and ball white, if desired. Push small pieces of pipe cleaner into the sides of the cones to make arms. Cut felt to hang over the pipe cleaners and glue in place. Add faces with black marker.

Funny Folks

F unny Folks are people-
pleasers. These fabric
fantasies can be filled with
polyester pellets or pillow stuffing
and then flopped down anywhere.

You Will Need
for each toy

½ yard (.50m) 45-inch (114.5cm) wide
orange or purple fabric, for body

¼ yard (.25m) 45-inch (114.5cm) wide
black and white striped fabric, for legs

6 x 8 inch (15 x 20.5cm) piece of black
felt, for feet

Thread to match fabrics

Scraps of green or orange fabric, for face

4 x 2½ inch (10 x 6.5cm) scrap of
purple or green fabric, for stems

Polyester fiberfill (or pellets), for stuffing

Heavy-duty paper-backed fusible web

Bottle of black fabric paint with
applicator tip

Tracing paper

Pencil

What to Do

Making the Body:

1 Enlarge and trace patterns below onto tracing paper and cut out 6 panels for the body.

2 Place 2 panels right sides together and stitch along one side using a $\frac{1}{4}$-inch (6mm) seam allowance. Begin and end seam $\frac{1}{2}$ inch (1.3cm) from each end of the panel. Continue adding each additional panel, in the same manner, to form a globe. When stitching the last seam, leave a 2-inch (5cm) opening in the middle of the seam line. Turn to right side.

3 Insert pellets (or fiberfill) through side seam opening and fill globe. Slipstitch opening closed.

Making the Legs and Feet:

4 For legs, cut 2 strips of striped fabric $11\frac{1}{2}$ x $2\frac{3}{4}$-inches (29.3 x 7cm). Fold each strip in half lengthwise with right sides together. Stitch long side closed using a $\frac{1}{4}$-inch (6mm) seam allowance. Turn right side out.

5 For feet, use boot pattern to cut 4 pieces from black felt. Place 2 pieces together and stitch around sides and bottom $\frac{1}{8}$ inch (3mm) from edge; leave top edge open. Repeat with remaining 2 pieces.

6 Insert a leg into top of each boot and slipstitch in place.

7 Place opposite ends of legs into bottom opening of pumpkin and slip-stitch closed.

Adding the Stem and Face:

8 Fold 4 x $2\frac{1}{2}$ inch (10 x 6.5cm) strip of green (or purple) stem fabric in half lengthwise with right sides facing and stitch together with a $\frac{1}{2}$-inch (1.3cm) seam allowance on long side and one short side. Turn right side out.

9 Pinch unstitched end together and insert into top opening of pumpkin,

slipstitch opening closed.

10 Draw freehand face features (or use one of the patterns for the Pumpkin Head Family on page 62) on paper side of fusible web and fuse to wrong side of face fabric. Cut out features, remove paper and fuse to

front of pumpkin with the tip of an iron.

11 Outline eyes and mouth with fabric paint and draw in teeth. For very young children who might peel off face pieces, reinforce features with stitching.

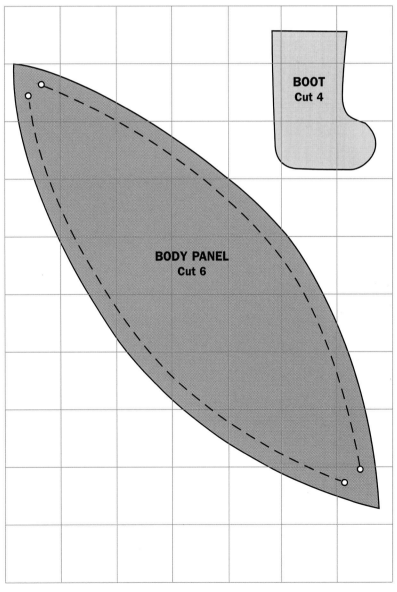

REDUCED PATTERNS FOR FUNNY FOLKS
Each square equals 1 inch (2.5cm).

Scaredy Cats Quilt

It will be love at first sight when your favorite child sees this Scaredy Cats Quilt. Children won't even want to leave it indoors when they go out to play. Border is machine-lettered but could be lettered with stencils and fabric paint.

You Will Need

3/4 yard (.70m) 45-inch (114.5cm) wide solid orange fabric, for quilt squares

1 1/2 yards (1.40m) 45-inch (114.5cm) wide solid black fabric, for quilt squares and border

2 1/2 yards (2.30m) 45-inch (114.5cm) wide orange and black patterned fabric, for piping and quilt back

Twenty 10-inch (25.5cm) squares of assorted Halloween-print fabrics (half with orange backgrounds and half with black backgrounds), for cat appliqués

40 small white buttons, for eyes (or use contrasting thread)

1 1/4 yards (1.15m) paper-backed fusible web, cut into twenty 9-inch squares

6 yards (5.50m) 1/2-inch (1.3cm) diameter cord, for piping

Black, orange, and white thread for stitching cats

White rayon thread, for embroidering lettering

Sewing machine with embroidery capability

High-loft batting

Pencil

Light-colored transfer paper

Iron

Optional: White fabric paint, alphabet stencils and stencil brush if you choose to paint lettering instead of embroidering it.

What to Do

Making the Quilt Blocks:

1 Cut ten 10-inch (25.5cm) squares from orange fabric yardage. Repeat with black fabric.

2 Enlarge cat pattern and trace onto paper side of each square of fusible web. (Image will be reversed on quilt.)

3 Fuse one square of fusible web to the wrong side of each printed fabric square. Cut out cat shapes, peel away paper and, centering carefully, fuse orange cats to black squares and black cats to orange squares as shown in photo on facing page.

4 Use pattern and transfer paper to transfer placement lines for button eyes and stitching lines for mouths on each cat.

5 Stitch button eyes in place at markings. Satin-stitch mouths over marked lines. If not using buttons, satin-stitch eyes.

6 Using a satin stitch, in a thread color to match cat, machine-stitch around the edges of each cat.

Assembling the Squares:

7 Stitch 5 horizontal rows of 4 cats together as follows:
Numbering the rows from the left and working from top to bottom, begin rows 1, 3, and 5 with a black square. Alternate black/orange/black/orange and stitch squares right sides together along the head/tail side edges with a 1/4-inch (6mm) seam. Begin remaining rows (2 and 4) with an orange square and repeat above procedure. On each row, press the seam allowances toward the black squares.

8 Place top 2 horizontal rows, right sides together and matching seams. Stitch along adjacent long edge with a 1/4-inch (6mm) seam allowance. Add each additional row, creating a checkerboard effect with the squares.

Making the Piping:

9 Cut a 45 x 55 inch (114.5 x 139.5cm) rectangle from backing fabric. Set aside. Cut remaining matching fabric into bias strips 1 1/2 inches (3.8cm) wide. Stitch strips together to make one strip, 5 1/2 yards (5.05m) long.

10 Fold bias strip around cording, wrong sides together, raw edges even. Using the zipper foot on your machine and thread to match fabric, stitch close to cord.

11 Machine-baste the piping to the edge of the quilt front (joined squares), keeping raw edges even and right sides facing.

Making the Lettered Border:

12 Cut 2 strips of black fabric 54 1/2 x 3 3/4 inches (138.5 x 9.5cm) and 2 strips of black fabric 38 1/2 x 3 3/4 inches (98 x 9.5cm).

13 Mark placement for lettering on each strip. Letters are 1-inch (2.5cm) high; "Scaredy Cats" repeats 3 times on each long strip and twice on each short strip. Begin and end stitching 3 inches (7.5cm) from ends of each long strip and 2 1/2 inches (13mm) from ends of each short strip.

13a If using a computerized sewing machine, refer to your instruction manual for programming procedure. Program "Scaredy Cats," thread top of machine with white rayon thread, use white sewing thread in the bobbin, and stitch words on each strip.

13b If using fabric paint, select the appropriate letters from an alphabet stencil and apply the words "Scaredy Cats" on each strip with a dressmaker's pencil. When you are satisfied with the spacing, stencil with white fabric paint.

Scaredy Cats Quilt

Adding the Border:

14 Center and stitch the 2 short word strips to the top and bottom edges of the piped quilt, right sides together, using a zipper foot attachment.

15 Center and stitch long word strips to long edges of quilt in the same way.

16 Lay batting out smooth. Place quilt back and quilt top, with right sides facing, over batting. Trim backing and batting edges even with quilt top edges. Stitch around with ½ inch (1.3cm) seams. Leave a 6-inch opening in one long edge.

17 Clip across seam allowances at corners. Turn quilt right side out, insert batting through opening.

18 To quilt, machine-stitch through all layers on inside edge of piping, and along seam lines between squares.

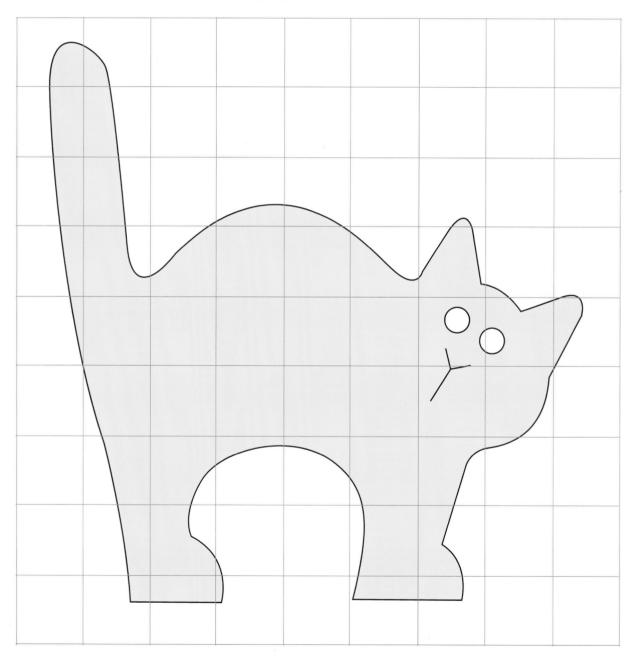

REDUCED PATTERN FOR SCAREDY CATS QUILT
Each square equals 1 inch (2.5cm).

Button-Trimmed T-Shirt & Socks

Enjoy shopping for clever mask, pumpkin, ghost, and word buttons and sew them into a yoke on a Button-Trimmed T-shirt, or add cats, and flying witches to the cuffs of socks.

You Will Need
for the T-shirt

Cotton or cotton-blend T-shirt

10 jack-o'-lantern buttons, ³/₄-inch (2cm) diameter

30 black mask buttons, 1-inch (2.5cm) long

2 sets "BOO" buttons

6 ghost buttons, ⁷/₈-inch (2.2cm) long

12 inches (30.5cm) ³/₈-inch (1cm) wide orange picot-edge ribbon

Threads to match shirt and black for mask buttons

Pins

Ruler

Optional: Dressmaker's chalk

What to Do

1 Prewash shirt to remove sizing.

2 Place the shirt on a flat surface. Insert cardboard or magazine into T-shirt to keep it from stretching during sewing and to keep pins and stitches from going through to the back.

3 Position jack-o'-lantern buttons evenly spaced (about 1½-inches [3.8cm] apart) around front of neckline and extending to shoulder seams. Mark shirt with pins or dressmaker's chalk and set buttons aside.

4 Find the center of shirt and starting at neckline, use pins or chalk to mark a straight line down the front for 5-6 inches (12.5 to 15cm). If the shirt has a ribbed texture, use a rib as a guideline. If not, use a ruler.

5 Place, mark and sew 4 black mask buttons, evenly spaced, along this center line. Add 4 more mask buttons on either side of top button and extending out to shoulder seams. Add 5 more mask buttons on either side of bottom button, extending upward to meet top row. Fill in remaining areas between top, bottom, and center rows with 4 more mask buttons on each side.

6 Cut orange ribbon in half and make two small bows. Sew one to each side, as shown in photo, and sew a ghost button to the middle of each bow.

7 Sew jack-o'-lantern buttons in place.

8 Try the shirt on and mark positioning for "BOO" buttons and remaining 4 ghost buttons (2 each side). Remove the shirt and stitch buttons in place.

You Will Need
for socks

Cotton or cotton-blend socks

2-4 buttons for each pair of socks

Thread to match socks

What to Do

Sew witch or cat buttons to sock cuffs. If you want a button on each side of sock, you will need 4 buttons. To decorate outside of socks only, you will need 2 buttons for each pair.

Critter Caps

Chenille yarn is used to crochet these cute Critter Caps. Let children help with making the faces by drawing the features on felt and cutting them out. These hats will fit most 4 to 6-year olds.

You Will Need
for each hat

One 3½ oz. skein chenille yarn in orange or black

Crochet hook size F/5 (4.00mm) or size required to obtain gauge

Sewing needle and thread to match facial features

For cat hat:
Pink and gray embroidery floss

Scraps of black, yellow, and pink felt

For Jack-o'-lantern hat:
1 skein green chenille for leaves, and a small amount brown chenille for stem

Small piece of black felt, for face

Gauge: 16 sc and 16 rows equals 4 inches (10cm) over sc with size F/5 hook

(To save time, take the time to check gauge.)

NOTE: These instructions use US terms and abbreviations (see page 139). For Canadian terms, see conversions on page 139.

What to Do

Hat: Beg at top of hat with black, ch 3 and close into a ring with 1 sl st in first ch. Mark beg of rnd.

Rnd 1: Ch 1, 9 sc in ring. **Rnd 2:** 2 sc in each sc around — 18 sc. **Rnd 3:** *1 sc in next sc, 2 sc in next sc, rep from * around — 27 sc. **Rnd 4 & all even rnds:** Work even in sc. **Rnd 5:** *1 sc in each of next 2 sc, 2 sc in next sc, rep from * around — 36 sc. **Rnd 7:** *1 sc in each of next 3 sc, 2 sc in next sc, rep from * around — 45 sc. **Rnd 9:** *1 sc in each of next 4 sc, 2 sc in next sc, rep from * around — 54 sc. **Rnd 11:** *1 sc in each of next 5 sc, 2 sc in next sc, rep from * around — 63 sc. **Rnd 13:** *1 sc in each of next 6 sc, 2 sc in next sc, rep from * around — 72 sc. **Rnd 15:** *1 sc in each of next

along side of hat for ear. Ch 1, turn. **Row 2:** Sc in each sc across. Ch 1, turn. **Row 3:** (Pull up a loop in each of next 2 sc, yo and draw yarn through all 3 loops on hook - dec made), sc in each sc to end of row. Ch 1, turn. Rep last row until 1 st remains. Fasten off. Work second ear at other side of hat.

To Make Cat's Face:
Cut 2 oval eyes from yellow felt about 1-inch (2.5cm) long, 2 pupils from black felt. Cut one triangle for nose from pink felt. Following photo, sew features in place. Using a backstitch or machine-stitch, embroider 3 gray whiskers on each side of nose and a pink mouth.

To Make Jack-o'-lantern Stem & Leaves:
Stem: With brown, ch 9 and close into a ring with 1 sl st in first ch. **Rnd 1:** 1 sc in each ch around — 9 sc. Continue even in sc until piece measures 1 3/4 inches (4.5cm). Fold piece in half and from right side, sc open end closed. Sew brown stem to top of hat.

Leaves (make 2): With green, ch 13. **Row 1:** Sc in 2nd ch from hook, sc in next ch, hdc in next ch, dc in each of next 7 dc, hdc in next ch, (sc, ch 2, sc) in next ch, working on opposite side of foundation ch, hdc in next ch, dc in each of next 7 ch, hdc in next ch, sc in each ch to end. Fasten off.

Tendrils (make 2): With green, ch 35. **Row 1:** Work 3 sc in each ch to end. Fasten off.

Finishing: Sew leaves and tendrils to top of hat.

To Make Jack-o'-lantern Face:
From black felt, cut 2 triangles for eyes, one for nose and a smiling mouth and sew features in place.

7 sc, 2 sc in next sc, rep from * around — 81 sc. Work even in sc until piece measures 6 inches (15cm) from beg.

Brim: Next rnd: *1 sc in each of next 3 sc, 2 sc in next sc, rep from * around, end 1 sc in last sc — 101 sc. Work even in sc for 4 rnds.

Next rnd: *1 sc in each of next 3 sc, (pull up a loop in each of next 2 sc, yo and draw yarn through all 3 loops on hook - dec made), rep from * around, end 1 sc in last sc — 81 sc. Fasten off.

To Make Cat's Ears:
Row 1: From right side, join black yarn to hat at any place along 3rd rnd, then working towards brim of hat, ch 1, work 8 sc evenly spaced

Cool Cats

Halloween-print fabrics are used to stitch these 13-inch (33cm) tall trick-or-treating Cool Cats. Ready for their own costume party, they're holding machine-embroidered felt goodie bags in their paws.

You Will Need

for each 13-inch (33cm) tall cat

$1^{1}/_{4}$ yards (1.15m) 45-inch (114.5cm)
wide Halloween-print fabric, for cat body

Polyester fiberfill for stuffing

2 buttons for eyes

Matching thread

Contrasting thread for facial features

Scraps of yarn, for whiskers

Tapestry needle, to attach whiskers

For costumes:

Scraps of colored felt to fit
the accessories of choice
(including 8 x 8 inches [20.5 x 20.5cm]
for each bag)

2 hook-and-loop disks for cat paws

One 17-inch (43cm) chenille
pipe cleaner for tail

7 inches (18cm) $^{1}/_{4}$-inch (6mm) wide
ribbon, for bag handles

Scraps of tulle, rickrack, and ribbon
for bows;

15 inches (38cm) of $^{1}/_{4}$-inch (6mm) wide
ribbon, for mask

Fabric glue

Fabric marker

Tracing paper

Pencil

What to Do

Making the Cat:

1 Enlarge and trace front and back pattern pieces, page 104, onto tracing paper. From Halloween-print fabric, cut one front and 2 backs. Using patterns on page 105, enlarge and complete half patterns for tail and arm/paw. Cut 2 arm/paw pieces and one tail.

2 With a fabric marker, transfer all pattern markings to right side of the fabric pieces.

3 Using a satin stitch, machine- or hand-stitch mouth/nose on the cat front as indicated. Hand-stitch button eyes in place at markings. (For very young children, embroider eyes as well.)

4 Fold each arm/paw piece right sides together and stitch with a $^{1}/_{4}$-inch (6mm) seam allowance, leaving straight end open. Turn right side out, stuff, and slipstitch closed. Pin arms between X marks on each side of cat front and machine-baste in place.

5 Fold bottom corners of cat front right sides together as indicated by arrows, and stitch with a $^{1}/_{4}$-inch (6mm) seam allowance. Turn right side out.

6 Fold tail in half with right sides together and stitch with a $^{1}/_{4}$-inch (6mm) seam allowance, leaving straight end open. Insert pipe cleaner into the tail, then stuff tail.

7 Baste tail onto one of the cat back pieces at marking, machine-baste in place. Pin backs right sides together and stitch closed with $^{1}/_{4}$-inch (6mm) seam allowance. Bring bottom corners of cat back right sides together and stitch in place as with cat front.

8 Pin cat front and back right sides together and stitch with a $^{1}/_{4}$-inch (6mm) seam allowance, leaving a 3-inch (7.5cm) opening in the bottom for turning. Clip into seam allowances at curves. Turn right side out, stuff, and slipstitch opening closed.

9 For whiskers, thread 6 inches (15cm) of yarn into tapestry needle. Insert needle into one side of the mouth and exit on the opposite side of the mouth. Secure near insert and exit holes with a dot of glue.

Making the Hats:

10 Enlarge and trace half patterns for hat on page 105 onto tracing paper. Include markings between brim and top, and between white circles for ears.

11 For black hat, cut one front and one back from black felt, including top and brim. Place hat pieces together and stitch along the outer edge of sides with an $^{1}/_{8}$-inch (1.5mm) seam leaving openings in the sides of the hat, as marked, for cat's ears.

12 For two-tone hat (see yellow and orange) separate hat and brim pattern pieces. Cut 2 tops from yellow felt and 2 brims from orange felt. Place one brim piece at the bottom edge of one top piece, overlapping edges by $^{1}/_{8}$ inch (3mm), topstitch pieces together for front and repeat for back. Complete as in black hat, Step 11.

13 For hatbands, embellish a $^{1}/_{2}$ x 8 inch (1.3 x 20.5cm) strip of contrasting felt with an embroidery stitch and glue in place as shown. If desired, make another embroidered strip into a bow and stitch or glue in place.

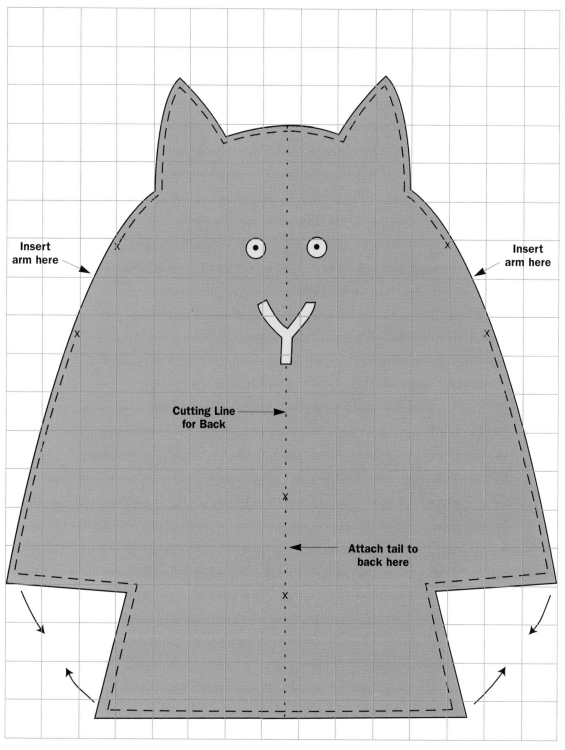

Insert arm here

Insert arm here

Cutting Line
for Back

Attach tail to
back here

REDUCED FRONT & BACK PATTERNS FOR COOL CATS
Each square equals 1 inch (2.5cm).

Cool Cats

Making the Trick-or-Treat Bags:

14 Cut 2 pieces of felt 4 x 4 inches (10 x 10cm). On one felt piece, machine-embroider a Halloween motif or letter the word "Boo" and satin-stitch over the writing.

15 Place bag pieces together, embroidered side facing in, and stitch along the sides and bottom with a ¼-inch (6mm) seam. Cut ribbon in half and hand-stitch to front and back top of bag for handles.

16 Attach hook side of hook and loop disks to inside of one arm and loop side of disk to other arm directly opposite hook disk. Slip bag over cat's arm and press disks together.

Making a Mask and Bow:

17 To make a felt mask, enlarge and trace pattern onto tracing paper and use to cut from felt. Cut ribbon in half and stitch a 7½-inch (19.3cm) piece of ribbon to each side of mask. Place over cat's face and tie in place.

18 For "hair bow," cut several 5-inch (12.5cm) strips of tulle, rickrack, and ribbon. Layer with tulle on bottom and ribbon and rickrack on top.

Tie a piece of yarn around the center of the strips to secure. Glue or stitch bow to cat's head.

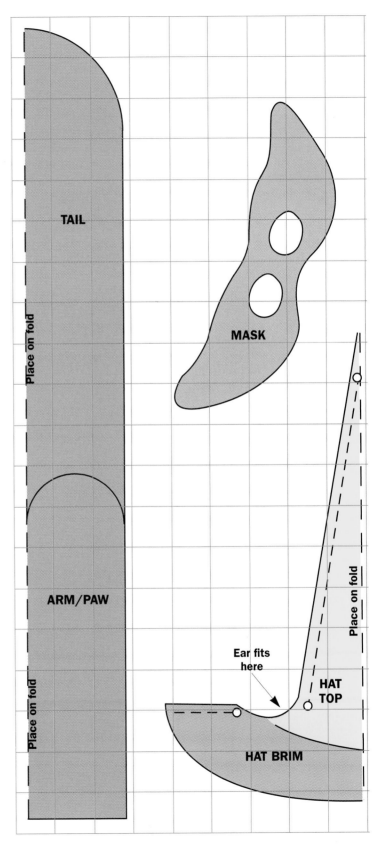

REDUCED PATTERNS FOR COOL CATS
Each square equals 1 inch (2.5cm).

My Three Witches

Great for gifts and party favors, My Three Witches are painted Styrofoam® cones "dressed" for the occasion. Make enough to line a mantel or a shelf. Although they are not suggested as toys for very young children because of their dowel broomsticks and arms, older children will want to create their own.

You Will Need

**Green Styrofoam® cones, 9 x 3⁷/₈
inches (23 x 9.8cm), for small witch;
12 x 4⁷/₈ inches (30.5 x 12.3cm)
for medium and large witches**

**One 9-inch (23cm) square black felt
each, for hats and sleeves**

**¹/₄-inch (6mm) wooden dowels for arms
and broomsticks; (12 inches [30.5cm]
for small, 13¹/₂ inches [34cm] for
medium and 15 inches [38cm] for large)**

Small black buttons for eyes, 2 each

Yarn for hair

**Olive green chenille pipe cleaner,
4¹/₂ inches (11.5cm) for each nose**

**Scraps of felt, for hatbands, bows,
cheeks, and mouths**

Black acrylic paint, for cone and arms

Tan acrylic paint for broomsticks

Paintbrush

Small amount of raffia for brooms

Small saw to cut dowels

White craft glue, scissors, pencil

Butter knife or wooden skewer

What to Do

Making the Bodies and Faces:

1 For medium witch, cut 1¹/₂ inch
(3.8cm) from bottom of cone.

2 Cut dowels as follows: for small
witch, two 3¹/₂-inch (9cm) arms and
5-inch (12.5cm) broomstick; for
medium witch, two 4-inch (10cm)
arms and 5¹/₂-inch (14cm) broomstick; for large witch, two 4¹/₂-inch
(11.5cm) arms and 6-inch (15cm)
broomstick. (Cutting foam and dowels
should be done with adult supervision.)

3 Paint cones black, leaving a circular area of green showing for faces.
Paint arm dowels black. Paint broom
dowels tan.

4 Cut pieces of yarn for hair. Tie a
strand of yarn (or string) around cone
just above green face area, mark and
score with pencil. Remove strand of
yarn. Place a line of glue on scored
area. Using a tool (such as a butter
knife or wooden skewer), tuck yarn
hair into surface of plastic foam
directly through the glue all around
the cone. Cut yarn into bangs at front.

5 For faces, glue on button eyes,
green felt circles for cheeks, tiny
red felt triangles for mouths. Cut a
4¹/₂-inch (11.5cm) length of pipe
cleaner, fold in half, twist together
and push wire ends into cone for
each nose. Bend the pipe cleaner
down at the end.

6 Push dowel arms about ¹/₂ inch
(1.3cm) into sides of each cone at
chin level. Remove, apply glue to the
ends, and reinsert.

Making Sleeves, Hats, and Brooms:

7 Cut 2 each black felt rectangles for
sleeves as follows: 1⁷/₈ x 4 inches
(4.8 x 10cm) for small witch; 2¹/₄ x
5 inches (5.7 x 12.5cm) for medium
witch and 2⁵/₈ x 6 inches (6.7 x
15cm) for large witch. Glue each
rectangle over dowel arm and close
to cone body. Then cut the bottom
edge of the felt sleeve at an angle
as shown in photo.

8 For hats, cut black felt brims as
follows: 4¹/₂-inch (11.5cm) circle with
1³/₄-inch (4.5cm) center hole for
small witch; 5-inch (12.5cm) circle
with 2-inch (5cm) center hole for
medium; 5¹/₂-inch (14cm) circle with
2-inch (5cm) center hole for large
witch. Pull the felt doughnut-shaped
hat over the tip of the cone down to
the hair line. Glue a narrow strip of
felt around the brim joint as shown
on small witch. Decorate with additional scraps of felt, if desired.

9 Cut 2 long strips and 1 short strip
of felt to make a bow. Add a small
circle in the middle, and glue bow
under chin.

10 For brooms, glue short lengths of
raffia to the end of the broom dowel.
Tie a longer length of raffia tightly
over the glued area. Trim ends of
raffia even.

CHAPTER SEVEN

For the Home

Even before the leaves start to turn or there's a hint of frost in the air, our thoughts skip ahead to the holidays to come. Beginning with Halloween, many people display decorations in every room of the house and adorn their offices as well.

We like to celebrate by visiting neighbors' homes, inviting them into ours, and participating in community activities. Schools, clubs and churches plan bazaars and other fundraising events.

Company's coming. That's why this is the perfect time to show how gifted you are by making—and exchanging—clever handmade accessories for the home.

No-sew picture frames, "quick-tuck" fabric pumpkins, and machine-appliquéd hand towels are a cinch to make and guaranteed to be bazaar best-sellers. Add cider and cookies to the shopping lists of supplies and turn these into perfect group projects.

An iron-on Fright Night Wall Hanging with matching pillows, painted Partytime Place Mats, Window Watchers, and a Mrs. Good Witch Tote Bag are just some of the many other enchanting choices.

Partytime Place Mats

F looring vinyl, available in home supply stores, is the easy-care ingredient for these Partytime Place Mats. Napkin rings and centerpiece ghosts are made to match.

You Will Need

**Vinyl flooring material,
18$\frac{1}{2}$ x 13 inches (47.3 x 33cm)
for each place mat;
4 x 6 inches (10 x 15cm) for each
napkin holder and centerpiece ghost;
6 x 12 inches (15 x 30.5cm)
for doorknob hanger (page 112)**

Household scissors (or a craft knife)

Yardstick

**Acrylic paints in the following colors:
pumpkin, clay, black, white,
green and gold**

**Paintbrushes: #10 flat, #6 round,
#1 liner and a $\frac{3}{4}$-inch (2cm) flat**

**Stencil brushes, 1-inch (2.5cm)
and $\frac{1}{4}$-inch (6mm)**

Black fine point, permanent marker

Clear acrylic spray sealer

Dark transfer paper

Small piece of sponge

**For each napkin ring:
24 inches (61cm) narrow
orange ribbon**

**Compass
(for doorknob hanger)**

Partytime Place Mats

What to Do

1 Working on the back side of the vinyl (this will become the painted top), measure and mark a 12 x 18 inch (30.5 x 46cm) rectangle. *Do not cut out at this time.*

2 The pumpkin pattern is given actual-size on the facing page. Enlarge the ghost pattern (right) 140% for the place mat. Trace and cut out one ghost and one pumpkin pattern, transferring all markings.

3 For a place mat, place the ghost pattern on left side of the vinyl rectangle, 2 inches from the top (as shown in photo on page 110); trace shape. Place pumpkin below—and slightly overlapping—the ghost (bottom of pumpkin should line up with the bottom of the place mat). When satisfied with positionings, trace outlines. Then flop ghost pattern and place in lower right-hand corner of place mat, with part of the body and one arm overlapping the edge. Trace outline.

4 Cut out the place mat, using household shears or a craft knife. (If using a craft knife, work on a protected surface or a self-healing mat.)

5 Using ³⁄₄-inch (2cm) flat brush, paint the entire surface of the place mat with 2 or 3 coats of pumpkin color paint. Dry completely between coats.

6 Fit the pattern pieces into the outlines on the vinyl mat. Insert dark transfer paper in between, then mark the pattern details onto the painted place mat. Draw freehand stars, and moon or refer to the patterns on page 57 and trace a moon and stars, randomly spaced, within the center area.

7 Begin painting by outlining the pumpkin, with a wide stroke, using the #6 round brush and clay-colored paint. Then, continuing with the same color and using the 1-inch (2.5cm) stencil brush, make two circles on pumpkin face for cheeks.

8 With white paint and #10 flat brush, paint in the ghosts on each side of the place mat. Using a ¹⁄₄-inch (6mm) stencil brush, add circles for cheeks with clay-colored paint.

9 With #6 round brush and green paint, fill in pumpkin leaves and stem.

10 With a flat brush, paint the moon and stars using gold paint blended with a little pumpkin paint.

11 Use the liner brush and black paint to paint eyes, nose, mouths.

12 For checkered border, cut a ¹⁄₂-inch square (1.3cm) of sponge. Dip sponge into black paint and use to dab paint in place. Begin with inside row and place checks ¹⁄₂ inch (1.3cm) apart. Repeat with outside row, alternating checks as shown in the photo.

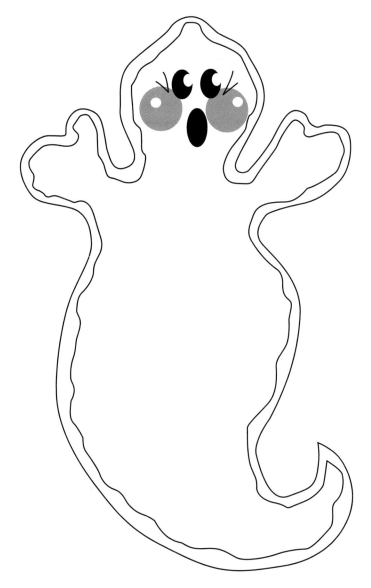

GHOST PATTERN
Actual Size for Centerpiece and Napkin Holder
Enlarge 140% for Place Mat

13 Add black paint dots to center of mat between stars and moon. Add small white dots inside eyes, nose, and cheeks of pumpkin and ghosts as desired. Allow all paint to dry thoroughly.

14 When paint is dry, use the marker to draw a freehand line—1 inch (2.5cm) from the edge—around top, bottom, and sides of place mat that don't overlap with ghost and pumpkin designs. Draw outlines for stars and moon, and add all fine detail lines to ghost and pumpkin designs.

15 Finish by sealing painted place mat with 2-3 coats of spray sealer.

For Centerpiece & Napkin Holder Ghosts:

16 Use the actual-size ghost pattern. Trace onto back of vinyl. Cut out as many as needed, following Step 4. Paint, transfer details and seal as indicated in Steps 8, 11, 13, 14, and 15. Arrange in a bowl of apples and fall leaves.

17 For napkin holders, poke a small hole in each side of ghost shape. Cut

two 12-inch (30.5cm) lengths of narrow orange ribbon. Pull the ribbon through the holes, knotting on top to hold in place.

For Doorknob Hanger:

18 Trace enlarged ghost and actual-size pumpkin motifs as for left side of place mat. Paint, decorate, and seal as above.

19 When dry, use a compass to draw a 2¼-inch (6cm) diameter circle in center of ghost. Cut out and fit over doorknob.

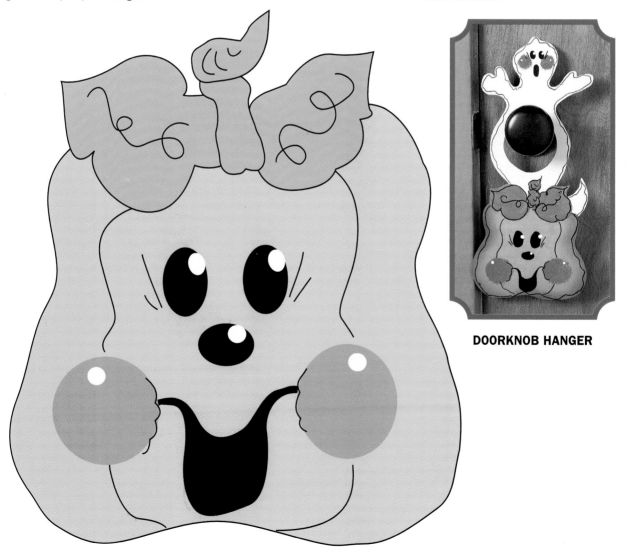

DOORKNOB HANGER

PUMPKIN PATTERN FOR PARTYTIME PLACE MATS AND DOORKNOB HANGER
Actual Size

Mrs. Good Witch Tote Bag

A store-bought canvas shopping bag becomes a wonderful Mrs. Good Witch Tote Bag with just a little acrylic paint. Personalize it by painting initials and/or the date in one of the stars.

You Will Need

Natural cotton duck tote bag at least 16 inches (40.5cm) in length, not including straps

Acrylic paints in the following colors: black, bright orange, beige, clay, olive and/or bright green, yellow-gold, white

Paintbrushes: 3/4-inch (2cm) flat, #10 flat, #6 round

1-inch (2.5cm) stencil brush

Black fine point, permanent marker

Light-colored transfer paper

Scissors

Tape

Pencil

Masking tape

Optional: assorted ribbons for bow on handle

What to Do

1 Enlarge the pattern on page 119 by 150%, until the witch measures 14 inches (36cm) from top of hat to hem of robe. Cut out pattern.

2 Center actual-size pattern on tote, and trace all around with pencil. Using 3/4-inch (2cm) flat brush, fill in outline with black paint. Let dry.

3 Draw freehand stars in assorted sizes on scrap paper. Cut out, position around witch on bag as shown and trace with pencil.

4 Align witch pattern over painted area, insert transfer paper, ink side down, between pattern and tote and tape in place. With a pencil, firmly go over outlines of main shapes including hatband, face, hands, and jack-o'-lantern. Remove pattern and transfer paper.

5 Using the #10 flat brush, paint the jack-o'-lantern with 2 coats of bright orange. (Let paint dry between each application and rinse brushes when changing colors.) With the #6 round brush and clay-colored paint, shade pumpkin shape by outlining with a wide stroke. Then with the stencil brush and clay-colored paint, make 2 circles for cheeks on jack-o'-lantern's face.

6 Use the #10 brush and one or 2 shades of green paint to fill in pumpkin stem, leaves, and the hatband. (We used olive for the pumpkin stem and leaves and painted the hatband a bright green with an olive stripe in the middle.)

7 Use the #10 brush to paint the witch's hands and face beige. You may need 2 coats to cover the black. To shade hands and face, outline with the round brush and a little diluted clay-colored paint.

8 Use clay-colored paint and the stencil brush to make circles for cheeks

and curvy brush strokes for bangs and hair at the sides of the face.

9 Using yellow-gold paint and #10 brush, paint small stars on hatband and fill in pencil-drawn stars around witch. Without cleaning the brush, use it with orange paint to shade the left side of each of the stars (except on hatband.) Use round brush and orange paint to add small polka dots between stars on hatband. Optional: Some of these stars are cut from vinyl scraps left over from the place mats and are secured in place with a glue gun.

10 When paint is dry, use marker to add details. (You may wish to re-transfer lines from pattern.) Outline stars on hatband, facial features on witch and jack-o'-lantern. Add lines for hair, veins on leaves and stem, and curvy vertical lines on pumpkin.

11 Using the round brush and black paint, fill in eyes and nose on witch and eyes, nose, and mouth on pumpkin. Let dry. Add white dots to facial features, as shown, for highlights. (The tip of a brush handle works well for this.)

12 Cut 3 strands of ribbon, tie together in a bow around handle as shown in photo on facing page.

Optional: You may substitute brush-on fabric paint if you plan to launder your tote bag.

Painted Window Watchers

Place this happy trio facing into a room or facing out the window to "watch" for company. Painted Window Watchers are tin cutouts. Vinyl flooring is used for the witch's arms and the jack-o'-lantern, which is held in place with magnetic stripping. Your local lumberyard will cut and groove a piece of wood for the stand.

You Will Need

Galvanized flashing tin sold in hardware and housing supply stores, approximately 20 x 30 inches (51 x 76cm) total

Caution: When working with metals, take extreme care. Corners and edges can be sharp and it is advisable to wear gloves. This is not a project for children.

Small piece of vinyl flooring, 10 x 10 inches (25.5 x 25.5cm), for pumpkin and witch's arms

Tin snips, for cutting metal

Household scissors, for cutting vinyl

Heavy-grit sandpaper

Metal primer

Acrylic paints in the following colors: pumpkin, white, black, clay, gray, medium green, lime green, beige, and gold

Paintbrushes: #10 flat, #6 round, #1 liner, #10 comb brush and ¼-inch (6mm) stencil brush

Black fine point permanent marker

Silicone glue

6 inches (15cm), ½-inch (1.3cm) wide magnetic stripping

Clear acrylic spray sealer

Dark and light transfer paper

Pencil

Optional: To make your own stand, you will need 12 x 4 inch (30.5cm x 10cm) length of 1-inch (2.5cm) pine and a jigsaw or table saw

What to Do

Preparing the Tin Shapes:

1 Enlarge the pattern for the witch on page 119 200%, to measure 17 inches (43cm) tall and the ghost pattern on page 118 200%, to measure 17½ inches (44.3cm) from tip of tail to tip of head. With dark transfer paper, trace enlarged patterns onto tin and outline with black marker, flopping ghost pattern so one faces in each direction.

2 Wearing gloves and using tin snips, cut out pattern shapes.

3 Sand surfaces and any sharp corners or edges. Clean and dry.

4 Use #10 flat brush to paint pieces with metal primer and allow to dry.

5 Paint witch with 2 or 3 coats of black paint, allowing to dry between coats and paint ghosts with white paint. Set aside.

Preparing the Vinyl Pieces:

6 Trace and cut pattern sections for the pumpkin and the witch's arms. Trace onto the back side of the vinyl, which will be the front side of this project (with one arm facing in each direction). Cut out with household scissors.

7 Using the flat brush, paint jack-o'-lantern with pumpkin color and paint arm fronts black with beige hands.

Decorating the Shapes:

8 To paint the witch (except for arms, hands, and pumpkin), use the light transfer paper and refer to Steps 4 through 11 in Mrs. Good Witch Tote, page 115.

9 To paint the details on the pumpkin

and ghosts, use the dark transfer paper and refer to Steps 7, 9, 11, 13 and 14, in Partytime Place Mats, page 112. Add strokes of gray paint

under hat brim as shown in photo.
10 After all painting is done and paint is dry, spray all pieces with 2 coats of clear acrylic sealer.

11 Glue arms into place. Glue two 3-inch (7.5cm) strips of magnet strip in an inverted T-shape onto back of pumpkin and position on tin witch.

12 Position figures in wooden stand as shown. Optional: To make your own stand, saw 3 grooves, ¹/₂ inch (1.3cm) apart, lengthwise, along the pine.

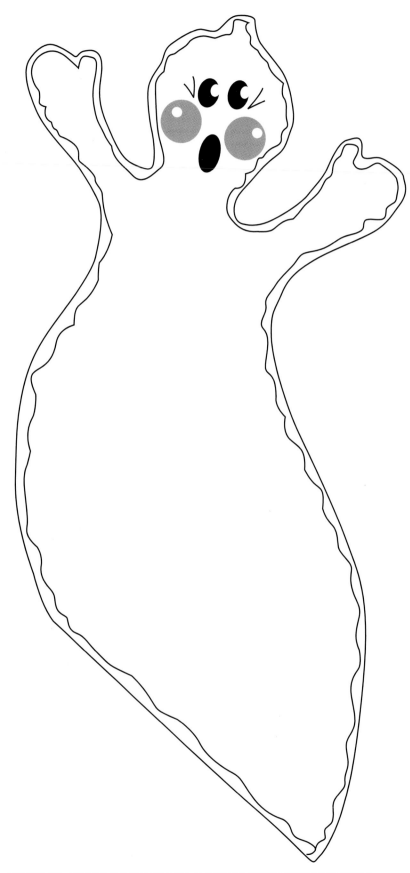

REDUCED GHOST PATTERN FOR PAINTED WINDOW WATCHERS
Enlarge 200%

REDUCED WITCH PATTERN FOR TOTE AND WINDOW WATCHERS
Enlarge 150% for Tote
Enlarge 200% for Window Watchers

Harvest Pumpkins

These Harvest Pumpkins are made using a "quick-tuck" method. Score grooves in Styrofoam® balls, then cut fabric pieces to cover each section and tuck fabric edges into grooves. Arrange in a bowl or basket on a hall table or use as a centerpiece.

You Will Need

Styrofoam® brand plastic foam balls, 4-inches (10cm) in diameter

⅛ yard (.15m) low-loft polyester quilt batting per ball

6 pieces of soft fabric (such as flannel or brushed knit) 8 x 3 inches (20.5 x 7.5cm) for each ball

Scraps of brown and olive green felt, for stems and leaves

Flat rubber bands

Serrated kitchen knife

Blunt-edge butter, table, or small putty knife

Indelible marker

Sharp pencil

White craft glue

Glue gun and glue sticks

Small, sharp scissors

Optional: Wrapped green florist wire, for vines

What to Do

1 To divide ball into 6 equal sections, wrap one rubber band around the middle and then crisscross with 2 more rubber bands.

2 Use the marker to outline the sections on the ball and to mark center top and bottom. Remove bands.

3 With a serrated kitchen knife, slice about ⅜-inch (1cm) from top and bottom of ball. Re-mark center of top and bottom and make holes ½-inch-wide and ½-inch-deep (1.3 x 1.3cm) at marks with the tip of a pencil. Re-mark section lines that were removed.

4 Using a sharp pencil, draw firmly along the section lines on the ball, creating depressions.

5 Enlarge the patterns to actual size and use the smaller one to cut 6 batting pieces and the larger one to cut 6 fabric pieces.

6 Glue batting onto the center of each section with glue gun.

7 To attach fabric to the ball using the "quick-tuck" method, center a piece of fabric over a section of batting as shown on facing page. About ⅜-inch (1cm) of fabric will extend beyond the incised lines on either side of the section. (You will be able to feel the lines through the fabric with your fingers.)

8 Beginning on one side of the section, place the blade of the blunt-edge knife on the fabric where you can feel the groove and push the fabric down into the Styrofoam at a 90-degree angle for about ¼ inch (6mm) all along the line. Repeat along the other side of the section. Strive to make the tension even along both sides of the fabric.

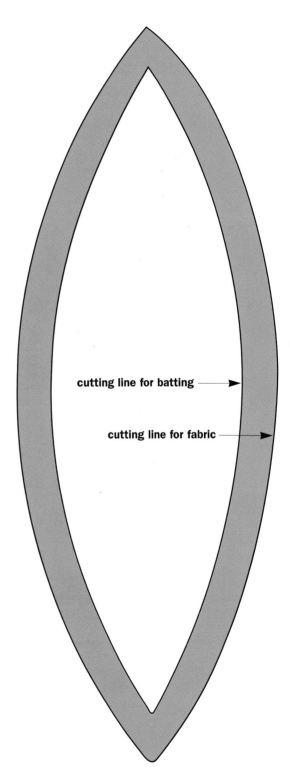

cutting line for batting ⟶

cutting line for fabric ⟶

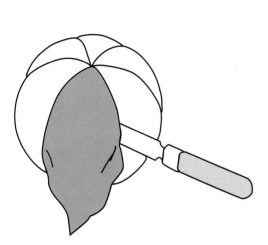

**"QUICK-TUCK" METHOD
FOR HARVEST PUMPKINS**

Push the excess fabric at top and bottom of ball into the holes. Snip away any excess fabric that sticks out along the vertical lines with a pair of nail scissors. Repeat with remaining fabric pieces until ball is covered. **9** For stem, cut a strip of brown felt 1½ x 2 inches (3.8 x 5cm), roll tightly from one short end and secure with white glue. Place a dot of glue into the hole at the top of ball and push stem into it. Cut out one or two green felt leaf shapes and glue next to stem. For vines, cut and twist 3 inches (7.5cm) of green floral wire around a pencil and push into the pumpkin at the base of the stem. **10** Cover bottom hole by cutting a ³/₄-inch (2cm) square of green felt. Place a dot of glue into the hole at bottom of ball and push the felt square ¼ inch (6mm) into the hole.

PATTERNS FOR HARVEST PUMPKINS
Actual Size

Fright Night Wall Hanging

This Fright Night Wall Hanging is made with fusible web. All you have to do is to cut out the motifs and borders and iron them in place.

You Will Need

½ yard (.50m) muslin, for background

⅛ yard (.15m) leaf-print fabric, for border

⅛ yard (.15m) each of solid or tone-on-tone print fabrics in brown, green, black, orange, gold and red, for design shapes

¼ yard (.25m) green, for border and binding strips

1 yard (.95m) paper-backed fusible web

⅝ yard (.60m) fabric, for backing, cut to 19 x 23 inches (48 x 58.5cm)

19 x 23-inch (48 x 58.5cm) piece of thin cotton batting

24-inch (61cm) transparent ruler

Precision rotary cutter

Self-healing mat

Fine point pencil or pen

Small, sharp scissors

Iron

Straight pins

Optional: Brown fine point fabric marker, to draw veins on leaves

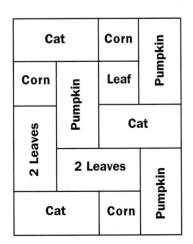

FRIGHT NIGHT WALL HANGING

What to Do

1 Pre-wash and iron all fabrics before cutting.

Cutting the Background and Leaf-Print Border:

2 Cut a 16 x 20-inch (40.5 x 51cm) piece of muslin for background. With a pen or pencil, mark a small dot at the edge of the fabric every 4 inches (10cm) around the perimeter.

3 Cut 2 strips of the border print 1½ x 45-inch (3.8 x 114.5cm). Trim again to two 20-inch (51cm) pieces and two 19-inch (48.5cm) pieces.

Cutting Narrow Brown Dividing Strips:

4 Cut a 2 x 17-inch (5 x 43cm) piece of fusible web and iron it to the wrong side of the brown fabric, following manufacturer's directions. Then, using the rotary cutter, ruler, and mat, cut 7 narrow strips each ¼ x 17 inches (6mm x 43cm). Then cut these strips into the following lengths: 2 pieces, 4-inches (10cm) long; 3 pieces, 8-inches (20.5cm) long; and 5 pieces, 12-inches (30.5cm) long.

Cutting Green Border and Binding Strips:

5 Cut a 5½ x 24-inch (14 x 35.5cm) piece of fusible web and iron it to the wrong side of the green fabric. Rotary cut four ⅜ x 24-inch (1 x 61cm) strips for borders and four ⅞ x 24-inch (2.2 x 61cm) strips for binding. Trim these strips into smaller strips as follows: 2 strips ⅜ x 19 inches (1 x 48cm); 2 strips ⅜ x 23 inches (1 x 58.5cm); 2 strips ⅞ x 20 inches (2.2 x 51cm) and 2 strips ⅞ x 24 inches (2.2 x 61cm).

Cutting Pattern Shapes:

6 Enlarge and cut out pattern pieces for motifs on page 124. Label pattern pieces.

7 Arranging pattern pieces by color, trace the following shapes onto paper side of fusible web: 3 black cats; 3

orange pumpkins with black features for each; 5 leaves (we used 3 brown, 1 gold and 1 green); 6 yellow candy corns, 6 orange candy-corn centers, and 3 pumpkin stems. *Patterns are the reverse of the way they appear on finished hanging.*

8 Cut apart sections and iron each to the wrong side of the appropriate color fabric. Cut out motifs on traced lines. If desired, draw veins on leaves with fabric marker at this time.

9 Remove the paper backing from all cut strips and motifs.

Assembling the Wall Hanging:

10 Using the illustration left, and the photograph as a guide, line up the brown strips on the muslin. To assure correct placement, line up the transparent ruler on the dots and center the appropriate brown strip underneath. When all the strips are positioned, iron them to the muslin.

11 Next, line up the two 20-inch (51cm) leaf-print border pieces touching, but not overlapping, the side edges of the muslin. Then line up the two 19-inch (48.5cm) leaf-print pieces along the top and bottom of muslin.

12 Add the 19-inch (48.5cm) narrow green strips to the border over the joining line at top and bottom. Place the 23-inch (58.5cm) green strips over joining lines at sides. Iron the pieces in place to complete the border.

13 Referring to the photo, position designs and iron in place as shown.

14 Sandwich the batting between the completed top and backing fabric. Pin around the edges. Crease the ⅞-inch (2.2cm) binding strips in half, lengthwise, with your fingers. Encase the quilt edges within the binding strips and iron from both sides. Use the 20-inch (51cm) pieces for top and bottom, the 24-inch (61cm) pieces for sides. Trim ends to make a smooth edge.

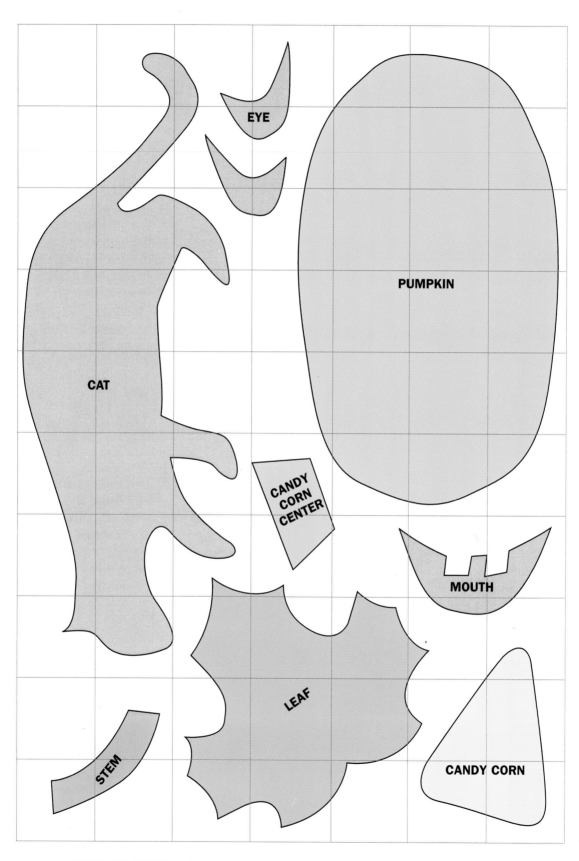

REDUCED PATTERNS FOR FRIGHT NIGHT WALL HANGING AND PILLOWS
Each square equals 1 inch (2.5cm).
Enlarge all 115%

Fright Night Pillows

These pillows repeat the same designs found in the wall hanging. Easy to make, you could place Fright Night Pillows on chairs all through the house. The motifs and technique can also be used to decorate a tablecloth or napkins.

You Will Need
(for 2 pillows)

¹/₂ yard (.50m) 44-45 inch (112-114.5cm) black fabric, for border, backing and designs

¹/₄ yard (.25m) plaid or fall-print fabric, for triangles to frame center

¹/₄ yard (.25m) muslin, for center diamond

Scraps of solids and prints, for motifs

¹/₄ yard (.25m) paper-backed fusible web

2 pillow inserts, 14 x 14-inches (35.5 x 35.5cm)

*plus the last 8 materials for Fright Night Wall Hanging

What to Do
(for each pillow)
Cutting the Pieces:

1 Using the rotary cutter and mat, cut a 6¹/₂-inch (16.5cm) square of muslin.

2 Cut a 7-inch (18cm) square of plaid; then cut it in half, diagonally, twice forming 4 triangles.

3 From the black, cut a 14¹/₂-inch (37cm) square (for back) and two 3¹/₂ x 8³/₄-inch (9 x 22.5cm) strips and two 3¹/₂ x 14³/₄-inch (9 x 25cm) strips (for front).

4 Enlarge the patterns on opposite page. Place pattern pieces of the same color together, right side down, on the paper side of the fusible web and trace around them. You will need 12 candy corns, 12 candy-corn centers, 4 leaves and either a black cat or a pumpkin with parts. Cut apart the fusible web sections and iron each to the wrong side of the appropriate color fabric. Cut on traced lines. Remove paper backing from all motifs.

Assembling the Pillow Top:

5 Use ¹/₄-inch (6mm) seam allowance throughout.

6 With right sides together, pin and stitch the long edge of a plaid triangle to one side of the muslin square. Repeat with another triangle on opposite side of muslin. Complete with remaining triangles. Press seams toward triangles. The piece now measures 8³/₄-inches (22.5cm) square.

7 With right sides together, stitch the 8³/₄-inch (22.5cm) black strips to opposite sides of the plaid. Press seams toward black. Stitch the 14³/₄-inch (37.5cm) strips to the remaining 2 sides. Press seams to black.

8 Using the photo as a guide, position the motifs and fuse in place.

Finishing the Pillow:

9 Turn and press under ¹/₄ inch (6mm) on the bottom of both the completed pillow top and the back. With right sides together, pin and stitch top and back on remaining 3 sides and fourth corner. Turn pillow cover right side out. Insert pillow form. Pin folded edges together and slipstitch closed.

Pretty-as-a-Picture Frames

These fun Pretty-as-a-Picture Frames are made from sheets of Styrofoam®. Cut out a center area for the picture to show through and then poke strips of Halloween-print fabrics and/or ribbons into the front surfaces until covered.

You Will Need

1 inch (2.5cm)-thick, Styrofoam® brand plastic foam sheet:
8 x 10 inches (20.5 x 25.5cm) for large frame;
5½ x 7 inches (14 x 18cm) for small frame

Assorted fabric and/or ribbon scraps

1 inch (2.5cm)-wide grosgrain ribbon to cover frame edges:
2 yards (1.85m) for large frame and 1½ (1.40m) yards for small frame

Utility knife with new blade

T square

Tacky white glue

Tool such as a knitting needle or barbecue skewer

Craft pins

Optional: Curling ribbon and self-healing cutting mat

What to Do

1 With a T square and pencil, measure and mark outside dimensions of frames, if not already cut to size. Large frame is 8 x 10 inches (20.5cm x 25.5cm) and smaller one is 5½ x 7 inches (14 x 18cm). To make center openings, mark 2 inches (5cm) from outside edges on large frame and 1³⁄₈ inches (3.5cm) on small frame. On a protected surface or a self-healing mat, cut along all marked lines. Set aside cutout center section.

2 Glue ribbon to interior and exterior edges of frame.

3 Tear fabric or cut ribbon into ½-inch (1.3cm) wide strips. Cut strips into pieces 2½ inches (6.5cm) long and angled at ends. If using curling ribbon, cut into 8-inch (20.5cm) strips and curl.

4 To apply fabric strips to front of frame, fold a strip in half, right sides facing, and twist twice at center.

Place a dot of white glue on Styrofoam and using the knitting needle or skewer, push the twisted area of fabric through the dot of glue and down about ¼ inch (6mm) into Styrofoam. Gently open fabric or ribbon strip to display right sides. Repeat until entire surface of frame is covered with assorted fabrics and ribbons.

5 Pin a picture to back of frame with craft pins.

6 For a standing frame, cut a wedge-shaped piece from Styrofoam scrap that was cut out for center hole. Glue to back of frame to make the frame stand up when tilted at a slight angle. To hang on the wall, rest frame on a nail at inside of center cutout.

Holiday Hand Towels

Appliquéd Holiday Hand Towels, or kitchen towels, with Halloween motifs stitch up in no time at all. Make several in an evening and try the same technique using bath towels.

You Will Need

1 dish towel for each

⅛ yard (.15m) orange pin-dot fabric for pumpkin

⅛ yard (.15m) black fabric for pumpkin face and cat or bat

Fabric scraps: yellow for mouth and green for stem

White thread to embroider cat face and whiskers and all eyes

Thread to match fabrics for appliqué

Paper-backed fusible web

Iron

Pencil

Fabric marker

Scissors

Tracing paper

What to Do

Making the Pumpkin/Cat Appliqué:

1 Enlarge pattern for pumpkin/cat on page 78 to 150%.

2 First, trace along outline indicated for shaded orange area only onto paper side of fusible web.

3 Then trace and cut out each remaining section of the appliqué design (one cat plus eyes, nose, mouth, and stem for pumpkin) separately. You may wish to label pattern pieces by color. Arrange pattern pieces by color, place right side down on paper side of fusible web, and trace. Cut sections apart.

4 Fuse each section to the wrong side of appropriate color fabric and cut out motifs on traced lines. *Patterns are the reverse of the way they will appear on the finished towel.*

5 Remove paper from each piece, one at a time, and fuse sections to towel, beginning with the orange shape. Fit other pieces in place. (See General Directions section on machine appliqué.)

6 By machine, satin-stitch around each section of appliqué with matching thread color. The stitches should enclose the edges of each appliqué piece.

7 Using a fabric marker or dressmaker's chalk, draw in the cat's face, whiskers, and the pumpkin's eyes. Machine-stitch over marked lines with white thread using a small zigzag stitch.

Making the Bat Appliqué:

8 Trace bat pattern (on page 78) onto paper side of the fusible web.

9 Fuse web to the wrong side of black fabric. Cut out, remove paper and fuse bat to towel.

10 Appliqué around edges as in Step 6.

11 Machine or hand-embroider eyes.

CHAPTER EIGHT

General Directions

Holidays are a time for friends and families to exchange ideas and try their hands at new—and old—talents. The pleasure of sharing knowledge and teaching one another new skills is as important as the final results.

For example, if you've never had the time to learn how to crochet, why not ask a neighbor or relative to give you a few lessons. In return, you can show her how to use the embroidery program on your sewing machine.

Detailed, step-by-step directions and patterns have been provided for each project shown in the previous pages. This chapter provides a review of sewing, crocheting, and crafting basics as a handy reference guide.

Transferring Patterns

The patterns in this book are presented in one of three formats:

1 Whenever possible, there is an *actual-size* pattern. In this case, simply place a piece of tracing paper over the pattern and trace. If it's a project that uses fusible web, the web is transparent enough that you can place it over the pattern and trace directly onto the web.

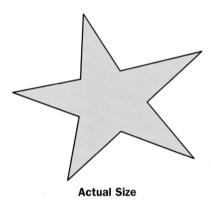

Actual Size

2 In other cases, there may be a *reduced pattern without a grid* and the directions will tell you what percentage to enlarge the pattern, for example "Enlarge 200%." Simply

Enlarge 200%

take it to a photocopier and enlarge accordingly. Using the example of 200%, you may wish to take a ruler to the copy shop to ensure that the size of the enlargement is double the size of the given pattern. The photocopy will then be your actual-size pattern. If the full pattern does not fit on one sheet of copier paper, you may need to divide the pattern into several sections; enlarge each section individually and then tape enlarged, actual-size sections together and label as necessary.

3 In some instances, there will be *reduced patterns on a grid.* This means that there will be lines running horizontally and vertically through the pattern. Refer to the scale, usually: "Each square equals 1 inch (2.5cm)" to determine how large the complete pattern should be.

To enlarge by hand, you will need a sharp lead pencil, a colored pencil, and a sheet of paper, large enough to fit the full-size pattern. Count the number of squares in each direction and refer to the scale to determine the paper size. On the large sheet of paper, draw a colored grid with the same number of squares, but make each square equal to the size

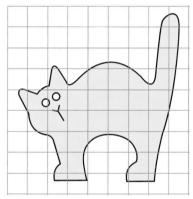

Each square equals 1 inch (2.5cm).

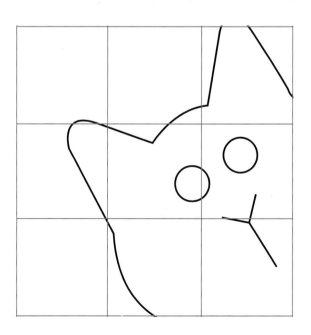

indicated in the scale, i.e., each square equals 1 inch (2.5cm). Working square by square, from left to right and top to bottom, use a lead pencil to copy whatever design lines appear in each square of the reduced pattern onto the corresponding enlarged square. Once you have completed this drawing, you may ignore the grid in tracing or cutting out the patterns. It is not necessary to copy the stitching lines or clip lines, just the outlines, or cutting lines, dash lines, fold lines, and 2-way arrows, which indicate how to lay the pattern out along the fabric grain or design lines. When there are several pieces, it is helpful to label what the pieces are.

To enlarge on a photocopier, experiment with the enlarging functions on the copier machine to enlarge the pattern until each square actually does measure 1 inch (2.5cm). You may need to break the pattern down into pieces if the full pattern does not fit on one sheet of copier paper; enlarge the sections and tape them together as necessary.

How To Complete Half Patterns

Long dash lines on a pattern indicate that half of a symmetrical pattern is provided. To complete the pattern, fold a sheet of tracing paper in half. Crease it and unfold it. Place the tracing paper on the half pattern with the long dash lines along the crease. Trace the pattern. Refold paper as before, and cut out the half pattern. Unfold the tracing paper to produce a full pattern. Transfer pattern markings from one half to the other if necessary.

Or, if you can see the pattern details clearly through the folded tracing paper, place the folded paper on top of the half pattern with the fold along the dash lines. Trace the pattern and then cut out. Unfold paper as described.

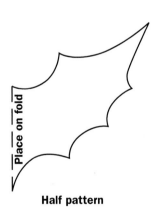

Half pattern

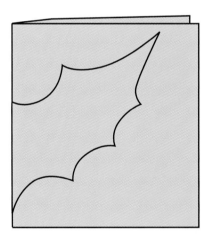

Refold paper with traced half pattern

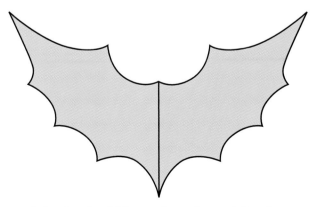

Cut out and unfold paper to produce a full pattern

Sewing Basics

Most of our projects are stitched by machine. Machine-stitching is not only faster, but it's sturdier for many projects, particularly when making something like a toy or a pillow. (However, if a sewing machine is not available you can almost always hand-sew, making short running stitches, or use backstitches with a double strand of thread.)

Sewing Supplies

In addition to a sewing machine and thread, there are several other sewing notions you will need when making a project.

Straight pins—Used to secure the pattern on fabric for cutting and to hold the fabric pieces in position for sewing. Round-head pins are easier to work with.

Scissors or Shears—Scissors are 6 inches (15cm) or shorter and shears are 6½ (16.3cm) or longer, with bent handles that are angled to make it easier to cut fabric. Scissors are used for trimming seams and threads.

Tape measure—Flexible measuring tool, generally 60 inches (152.5cm) in length. Useful for taking body measurements for costumes.

Marking pens and chalk—Used to transfer pattern markings to fabric and to mark casing and hem lines.

Seam ripper—small sharp hand-held sewing tool used to rip out stitches, when necessary.

Seam gauge—6-inch (15cm)-long metal ruler with movable plastic gauge in the center. Slide the gauge up or down, set at desired measurement.

Hand-Stitching

When sewing by hand, you will want to have a sharp needle, a thimble and perhaps a pair of small scissors for cutting threads. Select the needle size depending on the weight of the fabric; the larger the number the finer the needle, based on the thickness of the needle at the eye. Use a size 8 needle for medium-weight fabrics and a size 9 for lightweight fabrics. Choose a short needle for small stitches and fine sewing and a long needle for basting. Colored head straight pins are easier to see, and tweezers are helpful for picking out basting threads. Use all-purpose, mercerized sewing thread for most projects. If your fabric is cotton, use cotton-covered polyester rather than all-synthetic thread. Use a single strand thread about 20-22-inches (51-56cm) long (a little longer for basting) and a double thread for reinforcing areas that will be subject to extra wear and tear, as described above, as well as for sewing on buttons, snaps, and hooks and eyes.

Sewing by Machine

The references to machine stitching in this book assume straight stitch, about 10 stitches to the inch or 3 stitches to the centimeter, unless otherwise indicated.

We asked Nancy Jewell of Husqvarna Viking Sewing Machine Company for expert tips on perfect sewing machine performance and here's her advice:

• First and foremost, if you have not used your sewing machine in some time, review the instruction manual before you begin your project. Relearn the proper threading and bobbin winding procedures and how to set the machine for a particular stitch.
• Most skipped stitches are caused by a faulty needle. Needles need to be changed regularly, about every other project. If you cannot remember the last time you treated your sewing machine to a new needle, it's definitely time for a change.

Needle size is also important when constructing a project. If the needle breaks and/or does not seem to be penetrating several layers of fabric, your needle size may be too small. Use a size 12 needle for medium fabrics, a size 14 for heavier fabrics, and a size 16 for denim and canvas.
• If your bobbin thread (thread on the underside of your fabric) seems to be jamming or leaving a tangle of threads, check to see if your bobbin is inserted properly. Refer to your instruction manual for correct bobbin insertion. Once the bobbin has been inserted, test the bobbin before you begin sewing. Pull up on the bobbin thread by hand. The bobbin should turn counterclockwise. If it does not, then it has been inserted backwards.
• It is very important to use a good quality thread in your sewing machine. A rule of thumb when purchasing thread is that there is no such thing as a bargain when it comes to thread. Less expensive threads will often have thin and thick sections that will cause breakage and fraying when sewing. Thread that has been in your sewing basket for years is also not the best thread to use. Thread will rot and weaken over time and not perform well in your sewing machine.

Sewing Machine Feet

These are attachments that hold the fabric under the needle while sewing. Different feet are available for specific sewing techniques. Following are feet that are helpful when constructing projects in this book.

Zipper foot—This foot is used for applying zippers but may also be used for piping. The foot may be adjusted to sit on one side of the needle or the other, allowing the needle to stitch close to the cord of the piping or zipper teeth.

Piping foot—This foot has a groove that glides over the cord of piping and makes sewing piping nearly foolproof.

Satin-stitch foot—a presser foot with a groove on the underside. It is used for decorative and satin stitch. The groove allows the foot to glide easily over the stitches.

Open toe embroidery foot—This foot is shaped like a "U" and is opened in the front as the name suggests. This foot is perfect for appliqué as you can easily see the area you are stitching over.

Even feed foot—This foot has a set of movable feet on the underside that work in tandem with the feed dogs of the sewing machine to insure that both layers of fabric feed through the sewing machine at an even rate. This foot is used when sewing textured fabrics like fleece or layered projects such as quilts.

Seam Allowances

Measurements and patterns include seam allowances whenever necessary and will be indicated in the directions unless otherwise specified. When joining two pieces of fabric, pin them together with right sides facing and raw edges even. Sew pieces together, leaving the designated allowance between the seam and the raw edges. For example, a $\frac{1}{2}$-inch (1.3cm) seam allowance means to leave $\frac{1}{2}$ inch (1.3cm) between the seam and the edge. Press each seam as it's stitched, pressing seams open, for flatter results, or to one side—usually towards the darker color fabric, for more durable results.

How To Gather

Gathering is a method of sewing fabric in a way that allows you to gather it into soft folds. The fabric is reduced to about one third or more of its original width. For example, we used gathers on the skirts of the ballerina, angel and fairy princess costumes.

By Hand: Thread the needle with a long strand of thread, and pull thread ends even to create a double strand. Knot the ends together. Make even running stitches where you wish to gather, generally close to the raw edges of the fabric. Make stitches small for tiny gathers; make larger stitches for fuller larger gathers. As you stitch, you may slide the fabric toward the knot, to begin the gathering process. When you finish the line of stitching, keep the needle in place. Pull these thread ends and slide the fabric down toward the knot until the gathered fabric is the desired length. Fasten off by making a backstitch or two, and remove the needle. Distribute the gathers evenly along the length of the fabric.

By Machine: Set the machine for a long, wide, zigzag stitch, and knot one end of a long strand of heavy quilting thread or pearl cotton embroidery thread. Stitch over this thread, taking care not to stitch through the thread, except perhaps at the knotted end. Pull the opposite thread end and slide the fabric toward the knot. When the gathered fabric is reduced to the desired length, wrap the free thread end around a pin to secure the gathers. Distribute the gathers evenly along the length of fabric.

Sewing Terms

Backstitch—Secures the seam and prevents the seam from coming apart. Start and end each seam with a backstitch.

Satin Stitch—This stitch is used in appliqué. Adjust the machine to a short stitch length and a wide stitch width to create smooth continuous line of threads.

Topstitching—A visible, decorative way to sew something down, reinforce a seam, or hem. To topstitch, straight-stitch $\frac{1}{4}$ inch (6mm) from the edge, unless otherwise indicated.

Seam Finish—Used to prevent a woven fabric from raveling or fraying. Seams may be finished by machine using a zigzag or overcasting stitch or with a serger or overlock machine.

Serger—A sewing machine that trims, sews and overcasts seams in one operation. It is used in conjunction with a traditional sewing machine.

Serger Rolled Hem— A hem created on a serger. The stitch width is very narrow and a fine narrow edge is created.

Curved Seams

Curved seams are found on projects such as the Funny Folks toys, where several curved pieces are sewn together to form a sphere. They are used on the scarecrow's hat where the brim is sewn to the top and at the bottom edge of the sorcerer's hat.

When sewing a curved seam, extra care is required when guiding the fabric through the sewing machine. As the fabric passes under the needle, slowly turn the fabric, keeping the raw edge even with the seam guide. When pressing, it will be necessary to clip the seam allowance and remove some of the bulk, so that the seam will lie flat when pressed and turned right side out.

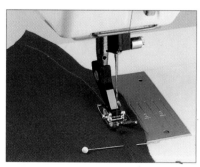

1 Place curved pieces with right sides together and pin-baste. Stitch along the seam line, guiding the edges of the fabric as you sew. Remove pins as you come to them.

2 Cut notches into the seam allowance from the edge of the fabric up to, but not through, the stitching line.

3 Press the seam open. Notice how the notches allow the fabric to draw in, so the seam will lie flat.

Casings

A casing is a "tunnel"—or opening—usually created by folding and stitching fabric so that elastic, drawstrings or a dowel can be inserted.

For our Buzzy the Bumble Bee and Jackie-O'Lantern costumes, casings were used at the neck edges for inserting drawstrings and at the bottom edges to insert elastic. Since the casing for the elastic is being sewn in a circle, only one opening is necessary. For a banner and other flat projects, there need to be openings at each end of the casing to hold a rod or dowel.

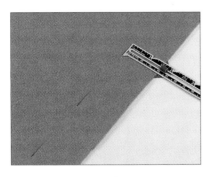

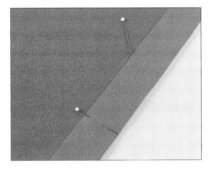

1 From the edge of the fabric, measure the desired width of the casing and mark fabric. The finished width of the casing should be 1/4 inch (6mm) to 1/2 inch (1.3cm) wider than the elastic, ribbon or rod going through it.

2 Fold fabric to wrong side along marked line. Press and pin-baste. Double-check your casing width with a hem gauge.

3 Machine-stitch close to the edge of the casing; remove pins as you come to them. Note: if the casing is being sewn in a circle, as with the bottom of the bee or pumpkin costume, leave a 2-inch (5cm) opening for inserting the elastic. On flat projects, such as banners, there will be openings at each end of the casing.

4 Trim any loose threads. Attach a safety pin or bodkin to one end of the elastic or ribbon. Insert the safety pin into the casing and work the elastic or ribbon through the casing. If using elastic, cut to desired length plus 1 inch (2.5cm). After elastic has been inserted through the casing, overlap the ends of the elastic by 1/2 inch (1.3cm) and secure with several rows of zigzag stitching, then ease elastic back into the casing and stitch the opening or the casing closed.

Helpful Hints for Casings

• To keep elastic from twisting in a casing, stitch through all layers, vertically, at side seams.
• When inserting elastic or a drawstring through fabrics that have been seamed together, stitch the seam allowance to the fabric in the casing area only, prior to sewing the casing.
• When sewing with felt or fleece, casings may be turned up without finishing the edge of the fabric. When using woven fabrics that fray, finish the edges by adding 1/4 inch (6mm) to the casing width and turn that extra fabric under before folding up casing.

Machine Appliqué

Appliqué is the process of applying shapes and designs to a background fabric. Although a satin stitch is the most common stitch used for appliqué, other decorative sewing machine stitches such as the feather stitch and blanket stitch are also appropriate.

Use larger, wider stitching on large appliqué pieces and narrow stitching on smaller appliqué pieces.

Fused appliqués, shown here, are the easiest to apply as they are first secured in place with fusible web. This prevents wrinkling and shifting when you are stitching.

Patterns for the appliqué designs in this book, are given in reverse so that the motif will appear in the correct direction on the finished project. (Fusible web is applied to the wrong side of the appliqué fabric, so asymmetrical patterns must be traced in mirror image.)

Helpful Hints for Machine Appliqué

• Test your satin stitch on a scrap of fabric before stitching appliqué to adjust the proper length and width. Length is the distance top to bottom between stitches and width is how wide the stitch is.
• Decrease the upper thread tension on your sewing machine to draw more of the top thread to the underside of the fabric, hiding the bobbin thread completely.
• Apply a layer of tear-away stabilizer to the wrong side of fabric for smooth satin stitching.
• Use a satin-stitch foot (which has a groove on the underside) to prevent a buildup of stitches.

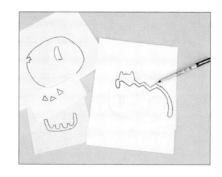

1 Trace each appliqué piece onto the paper side of paper-backed fusible web. Then cut around the appliqué outlines, leaving a small border of fusible web beyond the tracing line.

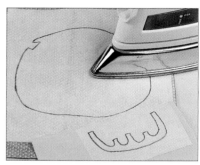

2 Place the fusible web, web side down, on the wrong side of each appliqué fabric, and press in place with a hot dry iron, following manufacturers' directions. Allow pieces to cool.

3 Cut out appliqué pieces along traced lines. Mark the placement of the appliqué pieces on the right side of your garment or base fabric. Peel off paper backing, and position appliqué pieces web side down on fabric then fuse in place.

4 Set your sewing machine to a satin stitch, (2.5–3.0 stitch width and 0.5 stitch length). Stitch around the raw edges of the motifs using contrasting or matching thread.

Machine Embroidery

Many of today's computerized sewing machines enable you to create professional-quality machine-embroidered motifs and lettering at the touch of a button. Follow the instruction manual for your machine and simply insert one of the pre-programmed embroidery cards available, attach the embroidery hoop, select your motif and stitch.

Machine embroidery was used for the lettering on the Scaredy Cats quilt, the goodie bags for the Cool Cats, the ballerina's leotard and the patches on the scarecrow costume.

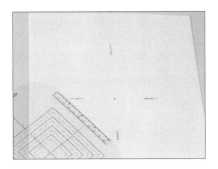

1 Place the embroidery template from your sewing machine accessories on the fabric. Using a fabric marker, mark within the grooves on the outside edges and center of the template.

2 Place 8 x 8-inch (20.5 x 20.5cm) square of tear-away stabilizer on the wrong side of the fabric. With the right side of the fabric facing up, place the fabric and the stabilizer in the embroidery hoop, matching the markings on the fabric with the markings on the embroidery hoop.

3 Place the embroidery unit on the sewing machine and attach the embroidery hoop to the embroidery unit. (Note: refer to the instruction manual for your machine when attaching the embroidery unit.) Select the desired embroidery motif, thread machine, and begin stitching.

4 Remove embroidery hoop from machine and remove fabric from hoop. Carefully remove tear-away stabilizer. Or to create an individual appliqué, as shown here, apply paper-backed fusible web to the wrong side of the embroidered fabric. Cut motif close to the stitching, and remove paper backing. Appliqué is now ready to be used.

Helpful Hints for Machine Embroidery

- Use metallic threads to add a festive touch to embroideries.
- Use transparent thread in the bobbin so threads will be less visible on the wrong side of your garment.
- Make a padded or quilted appliqué by placing a layer of batting between the fabric and stabilizer.
- Use stabilizer, a stiff tear-away backing, on the underside of the fabric when embroidering, to prevent puckering.

Hand Embroidery

If you prefer to hand-embroider details on some of your projects (such as faces on toys), here are some basic stitches that you might choose to use.

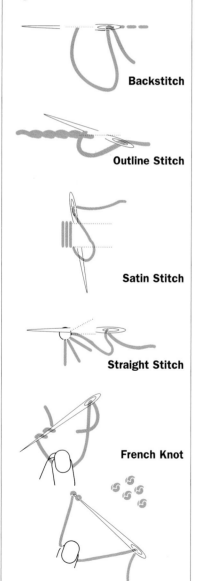

Backstitch

Outline Stitch

Satin Stitch

Straight Stitch

French Knot

Crochet Basics

Crocheting is a popular hobby and a versatile technique. All that's required is one tool—a crochet hook—and appropriate colors and textures of yarns. The yarns we used are Acrilan® acrylic yarns. Each set of directions will suggest the size crochet hook to use. As some people crochet tighter than others, the first step is to crochet a test swatch to be certain that your finished project will be the same as the dimensions given. The Critter Caps can be accomplished by most beginners. The Chenille Vest requires a little experience. One of the great advantages of crocheting is that it's easy to carry your work with you and add a few rows at a time whenever you can.

Checking the Gauge

Using the yarn that you intend to work with and the specified hook, make a chain at least four inches long. Work the stitches described in the gauge until the piece measures four inches square. Lay the finished swatch on a flat surface. Without stretching, squishing or altering the swatch in any way, place a tape measure or ruler across the width.

Count the number of stitches within the measurements given by the pattern gauge. Next, place your tape measure across the length of the swatch. Count the number of rows within the specified measurement.

If your gauge equals the requirements as given, fine. If not, use a larger hook if there are too many stitches or rows in your sample; use a smaller hook if there are too few.

Abbreviations

beg	=	begin
bpdc	=	back post double crochet
ch	=	chain
cont	=	continue
dc	=	double crochet
dec	=	decrease
fpdc	=	front post double crochet
hdc	=	half double crochet
rep	=	repeat
rnd	=	round
sc	=	single crochet
sl st	=	slip stitch
st(s)	=	stitch(es)
tc	=	treble crochet (Canada)
tog	=	together
yo	=	yarn over
* *	=	instructions between asterisks should be repeated as many times as indicated

Following a Chart for Crochet

Follow chart, such as the one on page 78, reading right side rows from right to left; wrong side rows from left to right.

To change color, complete last stitch of first color with next color. Drop first color to wrong side to be picked up as necessary. **Do not** carry colors across wrong side of work. Attach separate balls of yarn as needed. Fasten off colors when no longer needed.

Stitch Directions

yarn over: Wind yarn around hook.

single crochet (US); double crochet (Can): Insert hook in st, yo, draw yarn through st, yo, draw yarn through 2 loops on hook.

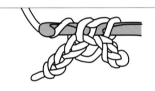

slip stitch: Insert hook through loop of edge, yo and pull through loop on hook.

decrease 1 single crochet (US); decrease 1 double crochet (Can): Pull up a loop in each of next 2 sc (dc), yo and draw yarn through 3 loops on hook.

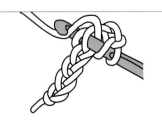

half double crochet (US); half treble crochet (Can): Yo, insert hook in st, yo, draw yarn through st, yo, draw yarn through 3 loops on hook.

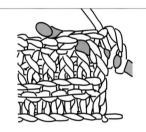

double crochet (US); treble crochet (Can): Yo, insert hook in st, yo, draw yarn through st, (yo, draw yarn through 2 loops on hook) twice.

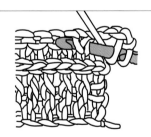

front post double crochet (US); (treble crochet, Can): Yo, from front insert hook from right to left around post of indicated st and complete dc (tc).

back post double crochet (US); (treble crochet, Can): Yo, from behind insert hook from right to left around post of indicated st and complete dc (tc).

Working with Styrofoam®

I f you can't find the exact size shape that is required for a project, purchase a similar shape slightly larger than what's required for your project and cut it to size. Plastic foam is easy to cut. For instance, if you need a 6-inch (15cm) square sheet, you can purchase a 12-inch (30.5cm) sheet, cut it in half and save the remainder for a future project. Or, if you need a 12-inch (30.5cm) sheet, you can purchase two 6-inch (15cm) sheets and glue them together.

Cutting: Styrofoam cuts easily with a serrated knife, hacksaw, floral knife or X-Acto™ craft knife. Wax the knife blade with an old candle for easier, smoother cuts.

Sanding: For smooth, round edges, "sand" the foam with another piece of Styrofoam. For large pieces, cut first and then sand the final shape.

Gluing: For a fast, sure bond, use a low-temperature glue gun. Hot glue guns can be used but might melt a small portion of the foam. (Please follow manufacturer's safety instructions when operating a glue gun.) White craft glue is a tried and true favorite for plastic foam; use florists' picks or toothpicks to hold pieces together while drying.

Painting: Paint with water-based craft paint or paints that are recommended for use on Styrofoam. When painting smaller pieces, insert toothpicks or wooden skewers in the back or bottom of the piece that you are painting so that the holes won't show and then insert the other end of the toothpick or skewer into a scrap of

Styrofoam or an empty egg carton in order to hold it in place while the paint dries.

Shaping: Press plastic foam with your fingers, roll it on a table, or texture it with tools. Try rolling it flat with a rolling pin.

Save the Scraps: When cutting pieces from Styrofoam sheets or other shapes, don't throw away the scraps; use them to create a base when arranging artificial flowers in opaque containers, or use in the bottom of pots when re-potting live plants, to create drainage. Spray-paint bits (or decorate with glitter glue) and string them together for garlands or children's necklaces. *As with any small object, keep very small pieces out of the reach of infants and toddlers who might be tempted to put them in their mouths.*

Using a Hot Glue Gun

A hot glue gun is a very handy tool to have. You plug it in, insert a glue stick in the back, and let it heat up for about 3 minutes. As the glue stick passes through the barrel of the gun, the heat inside melts the adhesive. When you push the glue gun trigger, liquefied glue is released from the nozzle.

The advantage of a hot glue gun is that hot glue bonds items almost immediately, as it cools and dries in seconds. There is no need to hold or tape items in place for several minutes until the glue is set, as with regular glues. You can apply a dab of glue, or keep your finger pressed on the trigger and draw out a line of glue. You should protect the work surface from any glue drips that occur. After glue is thoroughly cooled, remove any strings of glue from your project.

A glue gun is safe for adults to use—as long as you follow the manufacturer's instructions.

Some safety tips:
• Do not touch the hot glue or you will be burned. Keep a bowl of ice water handy and immerse a burned finger immediately to prevent blistering.
• Use a craft stick or toothpick to push items into the glue, or shift their position.
• If your glue gun does not have a stand, put it down on a sheet of aluminum foil.

Source Guide

The products used for the projects in this book are available in crafts, sewing and baking supply stores. In order for you to be able to duplicate the materials that we tested and used, here is the specific brand name information. If you experience difficulty locating any of the supplies that you might need, you can contact these companies for a distributor near you in the United States or in Canada.

All acrylic paints are "Ceramcoat" and clear spray sealer is "Satin Spray Finish" by
Delta
2550 Pellissier Place
Whittier, CA 90601-1505
(800) 423-4135

All plastic foam products are STYROFOAM® Brand products by
The Dow Chemical Co.
1610 Building
Midland, MI 48674-0001

All Halloween-motif buttons by
JHB International
1955 South Quince Street
Denver, CO 80231
(303) 751-8100

All fusibles are Pellon® products by
Freudenberg Nonwovens
3440 Industrial Drive
Durham, NC 27704
(800) 223-5275

Sewing projects were all stitched on sewing machines by
Husqvarna Viking™ Sewing Machine Co.
11760 Berea Road
Cleveland, OH 44111
(800) 358-0001

Chenille yarn is 100% Acrilan® acrylic "Chenille Sensations" by
Lion Brand® Yarn Co.
34 West 15th Street
New York, NY 10011
(800) 258-9276

All pumpkin-carving tools by
Pumpkin Masters, Inc.
P.O. Box 61456
Denver, CO 80206
(303) 665-7818

All self-stick hook & loop fasteners,
Velcro® USA Inc.
6420 East Broadway Blvd.
Tuscon, AZ 85710

Most Halloween-print fabrics by
V.I.P.
A Division of Cranston Print Works Co.
469 Seventh Avenue
New York, NY 10018
(212) 244-0794, x337 or 339

All baking tins, molds and cake decorating supplies by
Wilton Enterprises
2240 West 75th Street
Woodridge, IL 60517
(630) 963-7100, x320

Safety Tips

Here are some safety tips to keep in mind for your little trick-or-treaters:

❏ One or more parents should always accompany young trick-or-treaters.

❏ Stay in the neighborhood and map out a safe route to familiar homes for older groups of trick-or-treaters.

❏ Children should trick or treat only at familiar homes where the outside lights are on.

❏ Encourage children to complete one side of the street at a time and cross only at corners rather than darting back and forth, especially between parked cars.

❏ Make sure the children have flashlights—to see and be seen—and that they stay on well-lighted streets.

❏ Instruct children not to eat any treats until they get them home and feed them a meal or snack before they leave.

❏ Allow children to eat only those treats that are in unopened and original wrappers.

❏ Carefully inspect fruit and homemade goodies.

❏ Notify police if tampering is suspected.

❏ Make sure that children wear light colors or put reflective tape on their flame-retardant costumes, which should be short enough to prevent trips and falls.

❏ Children should wear safe, easy-to-walk-in shoes (this is not the time to try Mom's high heels).

❏ Use makeup instead of masks, which can obstruct a child's vision.

❏ Children should not enter a stranger's home, even when invited.

❏ Establish a curfew when children should cease trick-or-treating, perhaps by 7:00 PM.

❏ Children should not carry any sharp objects and never carry candles, even inside jack-o'-lanterns.

Acknowledgments

Project Consultants
Nancy Jewell and
Pamela Hastings
on behalf of Husqvarna Viking™
Sewing Machine Co.
for all sewing projects

Sharon Currier and Wendy Lovell
of Bozell Public Relations
for all Styrofoam® projects

Debra Garner
from Delta
for all painted projects

Jane Schenck
from Freudenburg Nonwovens
for all fusible projects.

Zella Junkin
from Wilton Enterprises
for Fun Foods

Kea Bardeen and
Kathleen Sexton
from Pumpkin Masters, Inc.
for the carved pumpkins

Signs of the Season
Smiling Scarecrow by Robin Tarnoff
for Husqvarna Viking; Grave Yard by
Frank Tompkins, Bittersweet
Branches by Linda Mills, Going Batty
Wreath by Annabelle Keller,
and Creepy Crawlies by Kathleen
George for The Dow Chemical Co.;
Black Cats and Yard Art Ghost by
Eleanor Levie; String Ghosts by Jean
Wilkinson; Yarn Ghost by Peg
Edwards; Pole Cat Banner by
Husqvarna Viking.

Costumes for Kids
Top Dog by Robin Tarnoff for Pellon;
Prima Ballerina and Patchy the
Scarecrow by Husqvarna Viking;
all others by Robin Tarnoff for
Husqvarna Viking.

Marvelous Makeup
Interview with Michael Thomas
by Mary Arrigo.

Pumpkins Etc.
Carved Pumpkins by James Egitto
for Pumpkin Masters, Inc.; Sparkling
Gems and Gorgeous Gourds
by Deborah Harding; all others
by Robin Tarnoff.

Fun Foods
All recipes and photos courtesy
Wilton Enterprises.

Festive Fashions
Chenille Vest by Nicky Epstein for
Solutia® Inc.; Entertaining Apron and
Denim Jacket by Robin Tarnoff for
Husqvarna Viking; Trick-or-Treat Shirt
by Trena Hegdahl for Pellon.

Toys & Gifts
"Haunted" Doll House, and My Three
Witches by Kathleen George for
The Dow Chemical Co.; Funny Folks,
and Cool Cats by Robin Tarnoff for
Husqvarna Viking; Scaredy Cats Quilt by
Robin Tarnoff for Pellon; Button-Trimmed
T-Shirt and Socks by Margot Hotchkiss;
Critter Caps by Nicky Epstein.

For the Home
Partytime Place Mats, Centerpiece
Ghosts, Napkin Holders,
Doorknob Hanger, Mrs. Good Witch
Tote Bag, and Painted Window
Watchers by Dorris Sorensen
for Delta; Harvest Pumpkins, and
Pretty-as-a-Picture Frames by
Kathleen George for
The Dow Chemical Co.;
Fright Night Wall Hanging, and match-
ing pillows by Judith Sandstrom for
Pellon; Holiday Hand Towels by
Robin Tarnoff for Husqvarna Viking.

Friends & Associates
My heartfelt thanks to the good
friends who generously shared
their candy corn, their pumpkins,
their experience, and even
their homes.

Rita Greenfeder
Eleanor Levie
Mary Merritt
Francis X. Morrissey, Jr.
Jean Wilkinson
Marita Thomas

And to Peter Mercurio for his
computer skills, to
Susan Brandt at H.I.A.
(Hobby Industry Association) for
her expertise on the crafts
industry, and to Michelle L. Keller
at Hallmark Cards.